PEOPLE TO KNOW

CHILDCRAFT

The How and Why Library

FIELD ENTERPRISES EDUCATIONAL CORPORATION

Chicago   London   Rome   Sydney   Toronto

Acknowledgments

The publishers of CHILDCRAFT—THE HOW AND WHY
LIBRARY gratefully acknowledge the courtesy of
the following publishers for permission to use
copyrighted illustrations. Full illustration ac-
knowledgments for this volume appear on page
366.

Esquire, Inc.: painting by Douglas Crockwell, page 259
(*top*), reproduced by permission of *Esquire* Magazine,
copyright 1945 by Esquire, Inc.
Time Inc.: photography by A. Y. Owen, page 215, courtesy *Life* Magazine, copyright 1956 by Time Inc.

People To Know

In this volume are forty-six unusual stories.
Read one of the stories, and you'll begin to see what is
unusual about it. Like all good stories, it begins with someone in
the midst of a difficult situation. Some problem confronts him;
some obstacle must be overcome. Then comes the climax.
Finally, we learn whether the hero of the story succeeds or fails.

Sometimes he succeeds, and sometimes he doesn't. That's the
way life is, and that's the way good stories are. But thus far,
although you have enjoyed reading a good story, nothing seems
particularly unusual. Then you notice a brief paragraph that is
separated from the end of the story—a short epilogue. Until
now you thought you had been reading a story about just
anyone—a fictional character. Suddenly, you discover that the
hero of the story really lived. Not only that, but you find that
he (or she) was a famous person—a person who has made an
important contribution to our culture. And you find that this
story is not fiction (although it is written in a fictional manner),
but that it really happened!

You have experienced a new dimension in storytelling. The
stories in this volume (and in Volume 12, too) are also
biographical sketches of some of the great human beings who
have lived on this earth. Sometimes the story takes place during
the hero's childhood; sometimes it is a story unrelated to what
the hero is famous for; and sometimes it is the story of the
hero's greatest moment in life.

And that is not all. In addition to having gained new
biographical insights, you have participated in a slice of history.
Not the history of dates and details (see THE WORLD BOOK
ENCYCLOPEDIA for detailed biographies), but the history
of human compassion, human courage, human intelligence,
the human spirit. To fill out the picture, a selected list of other
books to read appears at the end of most stories. And at the
end of the volume you will find a biographical chart showing
when each hero lived, where he was born, and why he was
famous.

There are many facts in this volume. But perhaps the most
important fact of all is that the great people who speak and
act in these pages are simply human beings. These are stories
of real people doing real things. The fact that they are also
about great people perhaps only makes us realize how
potentially great we all are.

The Editors

CONTENTS

VOLUME 13 *People To Know*

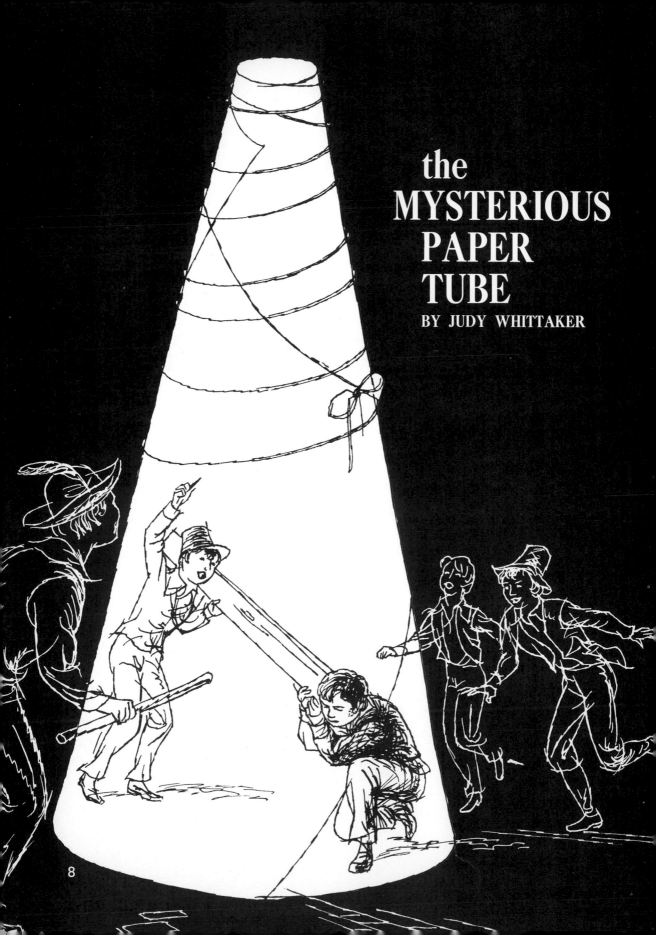

the
MYSTERIOUS
PAPER
TUBE

BY JUDY WHITTAKER

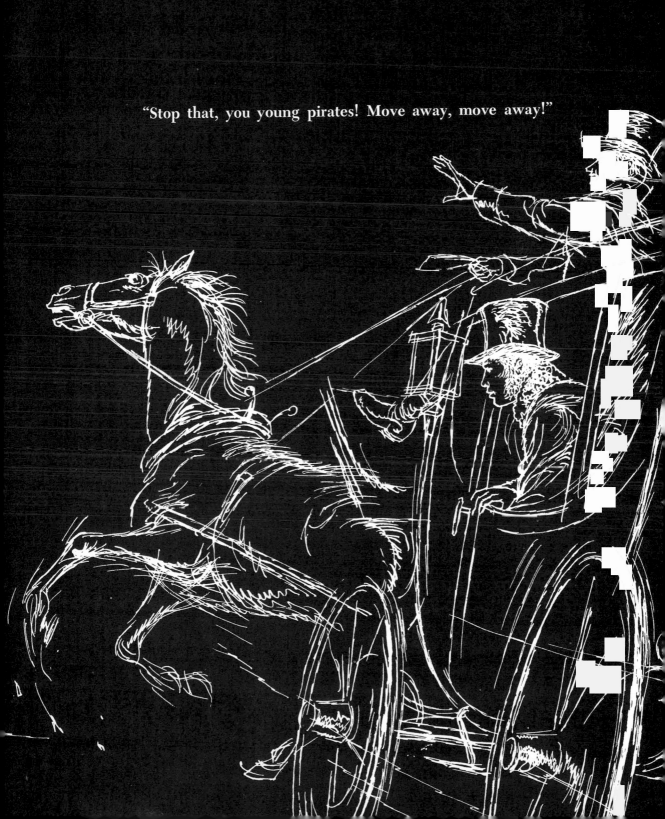

"Stop that, you young pirates! Move away, move away!"

The cab driver shouted angrily as he pulled his horse to a halt. "Go on, move, you little scamps! Can't you see I must get the doctor to his hospital?"

The man in black knee breeches and wide-brimmed hat thrust his head out of the cab window. "What is the matter, driver? Who is stopping us?" he said.

"I'm sorry, doctor, but just look at those boys. They're dragging a board across the street!"

Sure enough, there was a band of young boys pulling and pushing a large plank across the narrow, cobblestone street. They were chanting loudly:

"Scratch a board
With a nail . . .
You'll hear a sound
Never fail!"

The doctor watched with amusement. The boys were up to some trick, he thought. "It's all right, driver," he said, gathering his overcoat about him. "I'll get out here. It's only a short walk to the hospital."

The driver grumbled a few more words about the noisy boys, turned his cab around, and clattered away.

The doctor paused beside the boys, still wondering what they were playing.

"Come on, pick up the end of the board, now," the boys yelled to one of their companions.

A curly haired boy turned his back to his playmates and hoisted one end of the board to his shoulder. The end of the board rested against his ear. "You can't play tricks on me!" he shouted.

The boys grew quiet. Not a whisper was heard as one boy dug a crooked nail from his pocket. He stooped down and scratched the point of the nail along the far end of the board.

"I hear it, I hear it!" the curly haired boy shouted. "It sounds as if that scratching noise is right in my ear!"

So, that was it. The doctor smiled. I played that same game when I was a boy, he thought. But then he sighed. He was so busy now with his work that he could scarcely spare the time for even this short walk. He turned away and walked quickly down the street.

As the doctor pushed open the wide doors of the hospital, a group of young medical students clustered around him.

"Good morning, gentlemen," the doctor said. "I hope you are ready to learn more about healing the sick."

The students nodded and awaited the doctor's next words.

"Today, we will observe with our eyes, our hands, and our ears," the doctor said. "Then we will be able to decide with our minds the causes of sickness . . . and with work we will learn to cure."

The doctor walked quickly down the stone halls, from ward to ward, followed by his students. When he stopped beside a bed, he would speak quietly to the patient. Then he would feel the patient's forehead or use a thermometer. Sometimes he would use his fingers to tap on the patient's chest, a new idea in medicine, to find out if there was fluid in the lungs or chest.

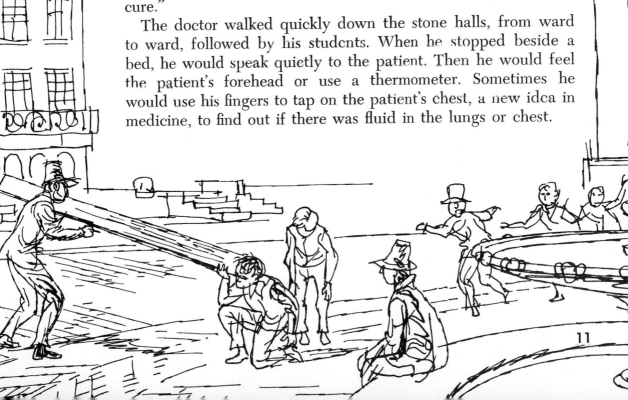

Often the doctor would drop to his knees beside a bed and put his ear on a patient's chest to listen to the heartbeats.

The watching students wrote in their notebooks the exact methods used by the doctor in his examinations. Later they would discuss the patients with the doctor to decide on treatment.

Silently the group of students followed the doctor into a large ward filled with girls and women.

The doctor stopped at a bed filled with a very fat young woman. She blushed scarlet when she saw them all looking at her.

"What is your name?" the doctor asked, trying to calm her.

"My name is Louise," she answered nervously.

"And how do you feel today?"

Louise smiled weakly. "Oh Doctor, I am so short of breath. It would be wonderful if you could help me."

The doctor saw that listening to Louise's heart beat would be very hard because she was so fat. Puzzled, he turned toward his students who were waiting to write in their notebooks.

"Gentlemen," he said, wondering what he could do next. How could he listen to Louise's heartbeats?

Suddenly the doctor remembered the game the boys had been playing with the nail and the board. Quickly he snatched a notebook from one of his students and tore out several sheets of paper.

The students watched him with amazement. Had the doctor lost his mind? What was he doing?

The doctor rolled the paper into a tube and leaned over Louise. One end of the tube was in his ear, the other on the left side of Louise's great chest. There! There! He heard the sounds of her heart, beating in an uneven rhythm.

"Today our ears have grown bigger and sharper!" the doctor exclaimed as he stood upright. "With this tube of paper, I can hear the heart beat louder and more accurately than I have ever been able to hear it before. The sounds of the heart and the sounds of breathing that I hear through this paper tube can open new worlds of study for all doctors. Perhaps we will be able to tell what sickness a person has by listening to these sounds."

The doctor turned to Louise with a glad smile. "And, Louise, now that I have heard your heart beat so clearly we can study *your* weakness better. Then we will know how to treat you. Soon you will be able to go home again."

The doctor who discovered the "tube of paper" in this story was René Laënnec. This story took place in Paris, France, not long after the United States became a nation.

With the "tube of paper," as he called his discovery, Laënnec listened to many different sounds made by the hearts and lungs of many different people. The "tube of paper" was the forerunner of the stethoscope your own doctor uses when he listens at your chest.

Laënnec worked very hard as a doctor during his short life. He died from one of the very diseases of the lungs he had spent his life studying.

More To Read

Great Men of Medicine by Ruth Fox Hume. Published by Random House, New York, 1961.

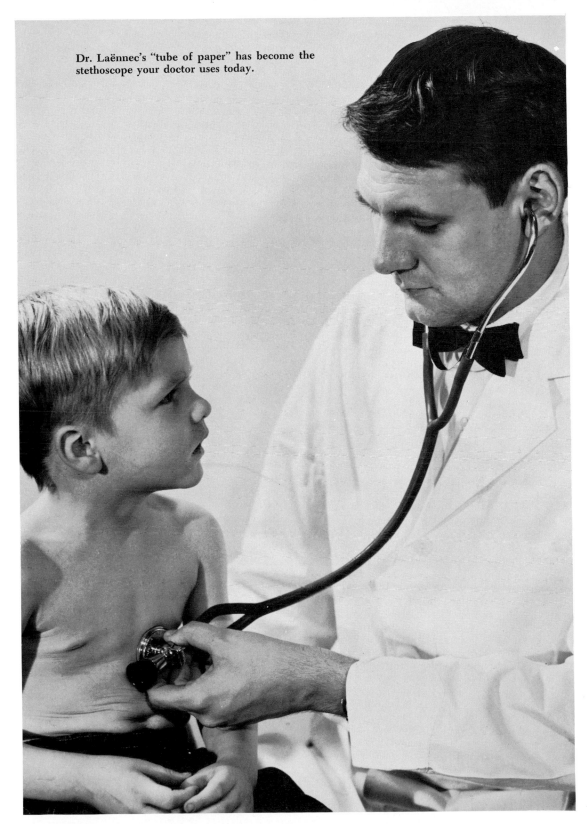

Dr. Laënnec's "tube of paper" has become the stethoscope your doctor uses today.

TRAPPED IN A HAYLOFT

By Katharine J. Carter

As the coach rumbled over the bumpy road, Gilbert and his friend stretched out their legs and leaned back in the uncomfortable seat. Suddenly, they both sat up straight. A horseman had come out from a side road and was following their coach!

"Hurry!" Gilbert called to the driver of the coach.

Gilbert knew that his enemies were trying to stop him from sailing to America. The Americans were fighting for their freedom. Freedom was something in which Gilbert believed deeply. He was going to America to help in any way he could.

On and on they went with the horseman following, but coming no closer. The coach squeaked and groaned.

Gilbert had disguised himself in shabby clothes. He was taking this back road in the hope that the soldiers who were searching for him would not find him. Not far ahead, his ship was waiting. But this horseman might be one of the soldiers looking for him. Would he fail now?

"If we are stopped, what can I do?" Gilbert asked his friend.

"I don't know. Let's hope the horseman won't recognize you."

But Gilbert was desperate. His ship was waiting for him. He could not be stopped now!

As if reading Gilbert's thoughts, his friend said, "Don't worry. If that man was looking for you, he would surely have stopped us by now."

"I've been thinking of that, too," Gilbert said. "But there is too much at stake for me. I can't be sure."

After another mile, the horseman turned into a wooded path.

"At last!" Gilbert said. "A few more hours and we shall be on board my ship!"

His friend added, "With luck we will."

Gilbert nodded in agreement. He knew that they would not be safe until they reached the ship. They continued for several more miles, bumping and creaking along the roads.

16

At sunset, the driver of the coach called back to his two passengers, "A mile yonder we will come to an inn. I'll stop there and rest the horses for the night."

"No!" Gilbert shouted. "We cannot spare the time! We might be recognized!"

"Sorry, sir, but the horses can't go on forever," the driver insisted.

"I'll hire fresh horses."

"The inn doesn't have any for hire," the driver said with a shrug.

"We need food and rest, too," his friend reminded Gilbert.

"All right," Gilbert sighed.

If only they didn't have to stop. The soldiers who were looking for him would certainly search the inn. And that would be the end of his dream of fighting with General George Washington in America.

Before stepping down from the coach, Gilbert looked around. There was no one in sight.

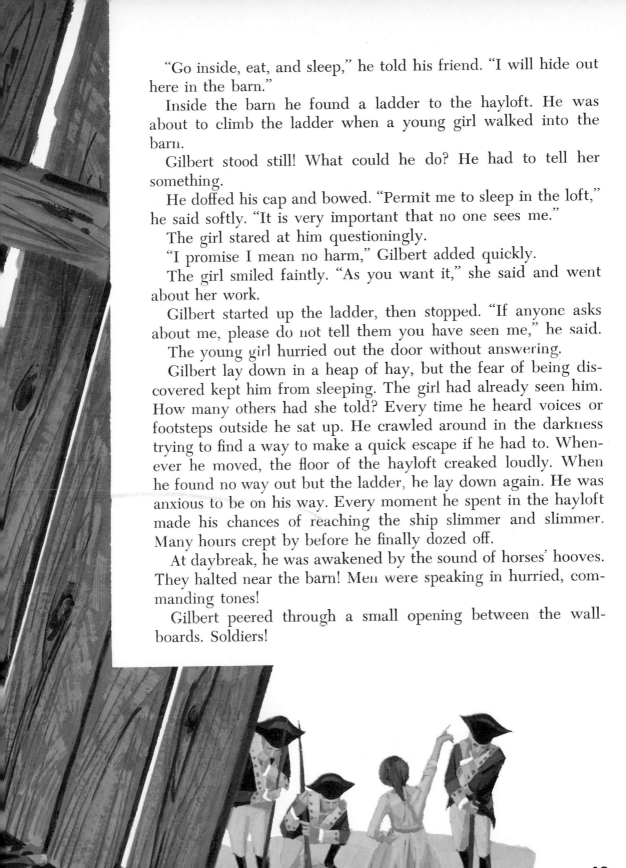

"Go inside, eat, and sleep," he told his friend. "I will hide out here in the barn."

Inside the barn he found a ladder to the hayloft. He was about to climb the ladder when a young girl walked into the barn.

Gilbert stood still! What could he do? He had to tell her something.

He doffed his cap and bowed. "Permit me to sleep in the loft," he said softly. "It is very important that no one sees me."

The girl stared at him questioningly.

"I promise I mean no harm," Gilbert added quickly.

The girl smiled faintly. "As you want it," she said and went about her work.

Gilbert started up the ladder, then stopped. "If anyone asks about me, please do not tell them you have seen me," he said.

The young girl hurried out the door without answering.

Gilbert lay down in a heap of hay, but the fear of being discovered kept him from sleeping. The girl had already seen him. How many others had she told? Every time he heard voices or footsteps outside he sat up. He crawled around in the darkness trying to find a way to make a quick escape if he had to. Whenever he moved, the floor of the hayloft creaked loudly. When he found no way out but the ladder, he lay down again. He was anxious to be on his way. Every moment he spent in the hayloft made his chances of reaching the ship slimmer and slimmer. Many hours crept by before he finally dozed off.

At daybreak, he was awakened by the sound of horses' hooves. They halted near the barn! Men were speaking in hurried, commanding tones!

Gilbert peered through a small opening between the wallboards. Soldiers!

19

His heart pounded as he strained his ears. "He must have come this way," he heard one of the soldiers say.

Another one replied, "Maybe he went back to Paris."

Beads of perspiration formed on Gilbert's forehead. They were looking for him, and he could not escape without being seen.

The door of the inn opened. The young girl came out and walked toward the well.

His heart pounded faster. Surely she would give him away.

One of the soldiers called to her, "Have you seen a coach carrying a young man in a uniform?"

Gilbert held his breath. Perspiration trickled down his face.

"A coach went up the road about an hour ago," the girl answered in a clear voice.

The men thanked her and rode away quickly.

Overjoyed, Gilbert rushed outside. He thanked the girl and clasped her hands gratefully.

His friend joined him in the yard. They decided not to take the chance of traveling by coach again. They saddled the two coach horses and galloped off toward their waiting ship. At last Gilbert was on his way!

Gilbert, the young man in this story, was the Marquis de Lafayette. He was probably called Gilbert because his full name was too long. It was Marie Joseph Paul Yves Roch Gilbert du Motier.

This incident took place in 1777, shortly after the outbreak of the American Revolutionary War. Gilbert arrived in America and joined General Washington's staff as a major general. He led his troops to several victories for the Revolutionary Army. He returned to France a hero.

Lafayette became a prominent leader in the French Revolution which started in 1789. He continued to fight for freedom until his death in 1834.

He was buried in Paris, but some Americans who appreciated what he had done for their country covered his grave with earth from Bunker Hill, the scene of an important battle in the American Revolutionary War.

Marquis de Lafayette

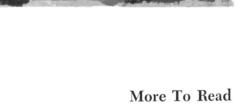

More To Read

Lafayette, Friend of America by Alberta Powell Graham. Published by Abingdon Press, Nashville, Tenn., 1952.

"TAKE A WHIP TO THAT PONY!"

The darkness was what Harry dreaded most. He awoke every day before sunrise to go to the coal mine. All day he worked in the blackness of the mine, seeing neither the hills nor the heather of his beloved Scotland.

Early one morning, Harry walked to the mine shaft. He filled his lamp and took his place on the elevator platform. Slowly, the platform moved down, deeper and deeper

By Mildred H. Willard

22

into the pitch-black mine pit. The ropes holding the platform swayed from side to side. Harry felt dizzy as the platform swung slowly, back and forth, and down, deeper and deeper.

Soon, all light from above was gone. The flicker from his lamp seemed about to go out. The taste of dust was in his mouth, and flecks of coal dust flew into his eyes. The pressure in the deep pit pushed against the boy's body. He struggled against the crushed feeling. Surely, this was like being buried alive.

The elevator platform jolted to a stop on the floor of the mine. Harry stepped off and started along the dark tunnel of the mine. His fingers groped along the damp walls as he felt his way in the darkness.

Suddenly, the darkness seemed to lift. The flicker in the lamp grew brighter, and Harry could see his beautiful silver pony, Wee Captain. Harry reached out and patted Wee Captain gently on the nose.

A loud shout struck Harry's ears, and a sharp whip cracked across the pony's back.

"Let's get going here," Harry's boss scolded. "Jump up, boy, and drive this pony. We've got lots of work to do today."

Harry climbed into the driver's seat of the wagon and started through the mine. Wee Captain and the other ponies were used to haul wagonloads of coal through the mine tunnels. The ponies pulled empty little wagons, called hutches, to the places where the men were digging coal. When the hutches were filled, the ponies would pull the load to the mine shaft where the coal was lifted to the surface and carried away.

Harry looked at the whip that was placed beside him. He would never use it on Wee Captain. Since the first day Harry had driven the pony, they had been friends.

Harry sang to Wee Captain as they went through the mine tunnel. He sang about the brave and strong Scottish heroes and about the beauty of the hills and lakes that he and the pony couldn't see. The songs seemed to take them out of the darkness and into the sunshine. He sang about the pretty wee houses in the glen and about the ships off the shore.

The other miners laughed at Harry. They thought he was silly to sing to a horse. As Harry and Wee Captain passed by a group of miners, one of the men called out to him, "Remember, Harry, ponies aren't people. They don't understand what you say. Someday, you'll have to whip that animal just like the other drivers do."

But Harry just smiled and went on with his song. He was sure Wee Captain could understand every word. Why, the little pony could even count the number of times they had been to the entrance of the mine.

The boy would say, "How many loads, Captain?" and the pony would answer by tapping on the ground with his right foot. The number that Wee Captain tapped out was never wrong. And when it was quitting time, nothing could make Wee Captain go back for another load after they had worked their full number of hours in the mine.

Wee Captain plodded along, never needing a spoken command. They picked up one load of coal, took it to the mine shaft, and went back for another load. All morning, they worked hard. Now they had only one more load to pick up before lunchtime. Harry sang a gay tune, and Wee Captain seemed to be tapping out the rhythm as he trotted along.

Suddenly, the pony stopped dead in his tracks.

Harry stopped singing and said, "Get on, Wee Captain. Why do you stop? It's not time for lunch yet. We've got another load to pull."

The pony twitched both ears slightly. He wouldn't budge.

"Please go on," coaxed Harry. "You're holding up the other drivers. They'll get mad at me."

Behind them, the other drivers were yelling, "You take a whip to that pony, Harry, or we'll come up and do it for you. That pony's a dumb, stubborn animal like all the others."

Wee Captain stood as still as a statue. Harry put his hand on the whip he had never yet used.

"Please go on," Harry pleaded again.

Instead of going forward, the pony pushed back against the wagon.

Suddenly, there was a loud rumble in the tunnel ahead. Bits of earth and stone came crashing down from the top of the shaft. Harry felt a rock strike his jaw. Other rocks were falling all around him. Wee Captain swung completely around in his tracks, pulling the wagon behind him.

Just as the pony turned around, the roof of the tunnel came crashing down. Huge rocks thundered to the floor of the mine. Dust and tiny pebbles sprayed against Harry and Wee Captain. But the pony scampered back through the passage. In a matter of minutes the passage was filled with stones. Harry looked with horror at the wagon. It was filled with jagged stones and rocks.

He jumped down from the driver's seat and ran to Wee Captain. He threw his arms around the little pony's neck and hugged him tightly.

"Oh, Wee Captain," he sobbed. "I'm sorry I was angry with you."

The other drivers rushed up and stared at the cave-in. If Wee Captain had gone on, they all would have been killed.

As Harry petted Wee Captain, he told the other drivers, "You were right. My pony isn't human. He's only an animal. That's why he could hear what we couldn't hear—the warnings of the cave-in rumbling above us. It's a lucky thing for us all that Wee Captain has such sensitive ears."

After the cave-in, which occurred in 1884 when Harry was fourteen, the other miners became friendly to Harry. They liked his singing and encouraged him to sing in local contests around Hamilton, the town in which he lived, and in Glasgow, which was nearby. He became well known in his area as a singer. Soon he was earning as much money by singing as he earned in the mines. He left the mines to become a professional entertainer.

The boy named Harry became well known throughout the world as Harry Lauder, composer and singer of Scottish ballads. Years later, when success on the stage had come to him, Harry Lauder went back to the mines in search of his Wee Captain. He wanted to present his beloved pony with freedom in the sunlight. But he was too late. Wee Captain had died in the pit. But Wee Captain had been well taken care of by the miners whose lives he had saved.

Harry Lauder wrote in his own life story, *Roamin' in the Gloamin'*, that he had forgotten many men and would forget many more, but he would never forget Wee Captain.

Sir Harry Lauder

A GIANT SEESAW

By Clare Thorne

The flatboat was stranded.

A tall, gawky young man stood trying to figure out a way to get it over the dam on which it was stuck. Since yesterday he and the rest of the flatboat crew had been trying to push the boat loose.

As they pushed, the young man could hear the laughter and loud voices of the crowd that had gathered to watch from the riverbank. It seemed as though the whole village of New Salem had gathered there.

"That boat is stuck as fast as a burr in a buffalo hide," someone in the crowd laughed. "They won't get it off till next time the river floods."

"The way that boat is taking on water, I'll bet you a dollar it sinks before they can work it loose," someone else said.

"I'll take that bet," another answered. "My dollar is on that young fellow who's telling the crew what to do. He's so tall, he can't get his breeches to cover the far end of his legs! Why, tall as he is, he could jump in, stand on the bottom, and push the boat free!"

It was hard to be laughed at, even though the tall young man knew that the laughter was not meant to be mean. So much depended on the success of this trip.

He had been hired to pilot the flatboat down the river. This was his first real job. He was on his own, out to make his way in the world. The owner of this flatboat was the first person to show enough confidence in him to treat him like a grown man. More than anything else he wanted to live up to that confidence.

But here, right at the start of the journey, he had made a mistake that might have ruined everything.

When they had come round the bend yesterday, they had seen the low dam that stretched across the river. They should have used their poles to slow the flatboat down. But instead, they tried to get up speed and slide over the dam.

Before they were halfway over the dam, there was an awful thud. The boat stuck so tightly that it wouldn't budge an inch. The front end of the boat tilted up and the back end down.

To make matters even worse, the cargo—barrels of salt pork, sacks of dry corn, and a half dozen live hogs—slid to the back of the boat to weigh it down even more. The back of the boat had sunk deeper. Water started spilling into the boat!

Now, if something wasn't done soon, the boat would start sinking.

Scratching his head thoughtfully, the tall young man walked around the boat trying to decide what to do.

"I should have eased her up to the dam as gentle as a mother with a new baby!" he said to himself. "Then, when she scraped, we could have shifted the weight forward and tilted her across."

Tilted her across!

Why hadn't he thought of that before? For a whole day and a night he had been straining his muscles. Why hadn't he used his head as well?

"Look here, boys, I've got an idea," he said to his crewmates. "Let's lighten the load a little. Unload the pork barrels!"

"We got nothing to unload into," one of the boys said.

"Just heave the barrels over the edge," the young man said. "They'll float, and the dam will keep them from getting away."

So one after the other, the heavy barrels were lifted out of the boat and rolled overboard with a splash.

The crowd gasped when they saw how strong the young man was. He rolled up a barrel and pushed it over in the same amount of time it took for the other two men to do the same thing, working together.

Soon the boat was emptied of everything but the water and the tied-up hogs. All three of the flatboatmen stood in the front of the boat. When their weight balanced the weight in the back, the boat began to tilt forward.

But it was tilting too fast! The flatboat was tipping over the dam like a giant seesaw!

As the boat swung over the dam, the water in the back of the boat surged forward. The three young men had to jump to the center of the boat to keep it from turning end over end.

31

And now, just when it looked as if they had it balanced, the hogs came sliding forward, snorting and splashing and drenching the three young men as they passed.

The crowd on the riverbank laughed till their sides hurt. This was better than a circus.

But the tall young man wasn't paying any attention to the onlookers. He moved calmly toward the back of the boat to balance the weight of the hogs. Soon the boat was balanced across the low dam with one end sticking over the edge.

"You have to hand it to that young feller," someone shouted. "He's got a cool head."

"It'll have to be even cooler to get that boat over in one piece," someone else said. "He's got to get rid of the water to lighten the load. It'll take him a week to bail the boat dry."

But the gawky young man had put his cool head to work on that, too.

"Anybody hereabouts got anything I could use to drill a hole?" he shouted in a loud cheerful voice.

A boy, who was fishing from the dam, spoke up, "Henry Onstot's got a tool for making holes in his barrels."

"Reckon you could show me where to find him?" the tall young man asked.

"Sure," the boy answered. He used his fishing pole to point out Henry Onstot's store.

The tall young man went to borrow the tool and was soon back and ready to work. He made his way to the front of the

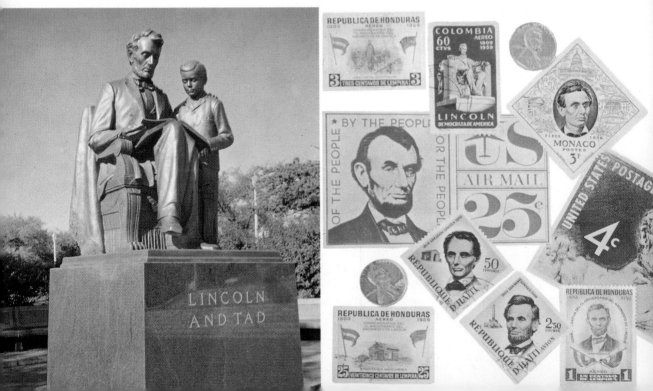

LINCOLN AND TAD

boat, knelt down, and drilled a hole. A minute or so later, he straightened up, gave the tool back to the boy, and sat down to whittle a plug of soft wood.

The crowd on the bank applauded as they realized what the young man was doing. There was a little stream of water running out of the end of the boat that hung over the dam. The boat was bailing itself without any effort on his part.

Soon the boat was dry. The young man plugged up the hole with the wood he had whittled. Then he and his companions eased the boat over the dam.

The problem was solved.

The owner of the boat, who had been watching from the riverbank, was as proud as if the gawky young man were his own son.

"I tell you that young fellow is going to amount to something," he boasted. "He's the smartest man in this part of Illinois! He's smart enough to be President someday! Mark my words!"

And the crowd roared with laughter once again.

But funny as it may have sounded, the words the owner of the flatboat spoke that day were destined to come true. For the tall man on the flatboat was young Abraham Lincoln, who was to become one of the greatest Presidents the United States ever had.

Shown below are some of the many coins and stamps from different parts of the world which honor Abraham Lincoln.

More To Read

Abe Lincoln Grows Up by Carl Sandburg. Published by Harcourt, Brace & World, Inc., New York, 1931.

Abraham Lincoln's World by Genevieve Foster. Published by Charles Scribner's Sons, New York, 1944.

Abraham Lincoln by Genevieve Foster. Published by Charles Scribner's Sons, New York, 1950.

Abraham Lincoln, Friend of the People by Clara I. Judson. Published by Follett Publishing Company, Chicago, 1950.

Abraham Lincoln by Ingri M. and Edgar P. d'Aulaire. Published by Doubleday & Company, Inc., New York, 1957.

the First Flight to Paris

By Joseph Martin Hopkins

Charles climbed into the cockpit of his single-engine plane and prepared to take off.

There was a sudden burst of sound as the propeller began to whir. Charles checked the instrument panel, then buckled his safety belt and pulled his goggles down over his eyes. He glanced at his watch. It was 7:52 in the morning. By tomorrow night he hoped to be in Paris!

A wave of his hand signaled the ground crew to remove the blocks from in front of the wheels. The plane moved forward with increasing speed.

The ground was wet and muddy. Charles had a terrific load of fuel on board to lift over those telephone wires at the end of the runway. I wonder if I'll make it? he thought. Should I stop?

The plane was going fast now, too fast for him to stop it. There was no turning back! Yet it didn't seem to be lifting enough to clear the telephone wires.

Charles sped closer and closer to the end of the runway.

Did he have room to take off?

The young pilot shuddered at the thought of what would happen if he tangled with those wires. There would be a fiery crash and almost certain death.

Slowly, the plane's nose lifted. Charles could no longer see the wires, but he knew they must be directly in front of him. He held his breath and urged the plane higher and higher.

Then he saw the wires as the plane swept over them and soared skyward!

The take-off had been successful, and Charles was now winging his way across Long Island, New York. Lovely estates and farms formed checker-like squares on the landscape below. Then came Long Island Sound. He looked down at the water and saw many different kinds of boats. He wondered where they had come from and where they were going.

Connecticut lay ahead. Charles studied his map and scanned the coastline below. He would follow the coastline to Canada before winging out to sea.

He checked his air speed. He was moving even faster than he had hoped.

The plane was performing beautifully. The weather was perfect. But the young pilot was growing worried. His journey was not yet four hours old, and already he was getting sleepy. This would never do. Somehow he must manage to stay awake. His very life, as well as the success of the venture, depended on it. The night before he had been so excited that he couldn't sleep. Now drowsiness was beginning to catch up with him.

It was noon. Busy with his charts and landmarks, Charles forgot how tired he was.

One o'clock! Lunchtime, he thought.

But he wasn't hungry. A full stomach would only increase his drowsiness. He contented himself with a sip of water from his canteen.

Now the wind was picking up. What if a sudden gust were to damage the wings of the plane and he were forced down? To allow for the extra weight of gasoline, he had not taken along a parachute.

But the wind finally died down. By midafternoon he had reached the Canadian coast. Then he was over the ocean. Charles lowered his plane until he was almost skimming the water.

Again his eyes began to close. If only I could keep them shut, he thought.

The water seemed so restful, so inviting. How can I possibly stay awake for so long? But I must stay awake! I must get to Paris!

Charles lifted the plane almost into some fluffy white clouds. Then he shook his head and body vigorously, flexed his arm and leg muscles, stamped his feet on the floor boards, and breathed deeply. Wouldn't it be stupid to spend months preparing for this trip, only to fall asleep and crack up? Charles asked himself. I must stay awake! I will stay awake!

Suppertime, he thought. But I'm not at all hungry. I'll take another sip of water. No, I'll wait until I'm really thirsty. This quart will have to last the entire flight.

The hours wore on. Nighttime! He passed through a blanket of fog, then a squall or two, and, finally, it was dawn. It can't be much farther now, Charles thought. But can I make it? I wonder where I am.

Then he saw something in the distance. As he came closer, the form took shape. It was a gull! Could he be that close to land?

He must be. There was a fleet of fishing boats just ahead. Land must be only a few miles away. But where was he? Scotland? Ireland? France?

Soon a rugged coastline, jagged as broken glass, stretched out below. Charles checked his charts. No mistake about it—he was flying over the southern tip of Ireland! A strong tail wind had sped the plane on its eastward journey. He was two hours ahead of time!

Everything seemed to be going well. At least he was heading in the right direction. He hadn't become lost at sea.

Charles began to feel better now. He was no longer drowsy.

Then Ireland was behind him. Rising from the sea ahead were the straight, sheer cliffs of Cornwall, England.

Only an hour to the coast of France! Looks like I'll make it by dark, he thought.

He was over the English Channel. Dozens of ships, from small fishing crafts to huge ocean liners, dotted the seascape below. Then at last he was over France!

An hour later he reached into a brown paper sack and pulled out a sandwich—his first food since leaving New York. He uncorked his canteen. No need to save water now.

First, he saw a glow of light in the distance. Next, the thin skeleton of the Eiffel Tower loomed on the horizon. Then the outlines of streets and buildings took shape.

Charles circled the Eiffel Tower, then headed northeast in search of the airport. But no sweeping beam of light, no rows of red and green boundary lights were visible. How could he land without lights?

But wait! There were some dim lights to his left. He circled over to have a look.

It certainly looks like an airfield, Charles thought. But where are the floodlights? I'll have a hard time landing without them.

Charles brought his plane lower. Now he could see the huge hangars jutting into the darkness.

Charles circled the airfield several times. Surely, by this time they would know that he wanted to land. If they weren't going to turn on any more lights, he would have to go ahead and land anyway. He couldn't stay up there forever.

The plane glided down. Now Charles could see a long line of cars jammed together along one side of the field.

Charles lowered the plane gently, feeling for the runway with his landing wheels. If only he could see! How could he land in the dark?

At last the landing wheels touched the ground. The plane rolled through the shadowy blackness. A perfect landing!

As Charles began to taxi toward the hangar area, hundreds of figures came running toward the plane.

He turned off the engine switch and started to crawl out of the cockpit. He was surrounded by a crowd of cheering people. They lifted him to their shoulders and carried him off the field in triumph.

Charles, the young pilot in this story, was Charles Augustus Lindbergh, the first man to fly alone from New York to Paris without stopping along the way.

When Charles Lindbergh took off from New York that morning in 1927, he was trying to do something no one had done before. He knew it would be only he and his plane against thousands of miles of land, ocean, and weather. Once he was in the air anything could happen. If he hadn't reached Paris safely, Charles Lindbergh would have been just another pilot who risked his life for a daring stunt and failed. But Lindbergh made it to Paris and became a hero. He landed in Paris almost a day and a half after his take-off.

We owe thanks to men like Charles Lindbergh who risk their lives for the sake of progress.

You can see Lindbergh's plane, *The Spirit of St. Louis,* if you visit the Smithsonian Institution in Washington, D.C.

More To Read

Ride on the Wind by Alice Dalgliesh. Published by Charles Scribner's Sons, New York, 1956.

THE HANDSOMEST

By Clarice Stetter

Tom hurried to the livestock market. He approached the man in charge of selling pigs and said, "I want to buy two of your largest and fattest porkers."

The livestock man looked Tom over from head to foot. Tom didn't look any older than twenty. He didn't look like the usual businessman who came to the market to buy pigs. But he certainly seemed to know what he wanted.

"I can give you two very fine porkers," the man answered. "How about these two over here?"

40

PIGS IN TOWN

The man turned and led Tom to a nearby pigpen. In one corner, wallowing in the mud, were two of the fattest pigs Tom had ever seen.

Tom's eyes widened with delight. "They're just right. I'll take them."

The man nodded his approval. "They're fine porkers. You'll get yourself a good supply of bacon from these two."

Tom smiled to himself as he paid for the pigs. The livestock man didn't know it, but Tom hoped these two pigs were going to

41

sell a lot of bacon for him.

When he got back to his grocery store, Tom approached his newly purchased pigs with a scrub brush and a pail of soapy water. He was going to make them the handsomest pigs in town.

He scrubbed and scrubbed. And the pigs squealed and squealed. Soon there wasn't a speck of dirt on either pig. Then Tom polished them until they shone. He attached tassels to their curly tails. Finally, he tied a pink ribbon around the neck of one pig and a blue ribbon around the neck of the other. Now the pigs were indeed handsome!

Next Tom hired a tall redheaded Irishman to take the pigs for a walk. The Irishman wore knee breeches, a cutaway coat, and billycock hat. He began parading the two pigs down a street some distance from Tom's store. They made quite a sight.

People turned to stare. They stopped and laughed at the fat, waddling pigs.

More and more people gathered along the street to see what all the commotion was about. They nudged each other and laughed. "Look at what's written on the sides of the pigs," one man called.

Other people stopped to read. There, painted in large letters on the sides of the two pigs, was the name of Tom's store and the words, "The best shop in town for Irish bacon."

Everyone stopped to look at the pigs and many began to follow this strange procession through the streets of town.

Suddenly, the pigs decided to take a rest. They came to an abrupt stop and flopped down on their sides right in the middle of the street. The Irishman who was walking close behind them almost fell on top of the two huge porkers.

The crowd let out a roar of laughter. Everyone moved in closer to see what would happen next. The Irishman tugged and pulled at the pigs. The pigs grunted loudly. But they didn't move. Some people shouted words of encouragement to the Irishman. Others cheered for the pigs.

More and more people crowded around to watch the antics of the Irishman and his pigs. Then suddenly, just as abruptly as they had lain down, the pigs decided to be on their way. With several loud snorts and grunts they rolled over and stood upright. The crowd let out a cheer. Waving his hat in the air, the Irishman started off once again down the street.

Once again the crowd followed behind them. The people laughed and joked as they walked along. They called to others to come and see the Irishman and his pigs. The crowd grew larger and larger. Everyone wanted to know where the pigs were leading them.

Suddenly, they found themselves in front of Tom's small grocery store. A large artificial ham hung over the door of the shop. The windows were newly washed and sparkling brightly. Inside they could see carefully arranged rows of eggs, bacon, and butter.

"So this is the store," someone said. "Well, let's go in and find out if the owner's bacon is as good as he says it is."

Tom stood in the doorway smiling. His idea had worked. The pigs were selling bacon for him already.

Tom, the young store owner in this story, later became known as Sir Thomas Lipton. This story took place in Glasgow, Scotland.

Not only did Tom's sense of humor bring him a lot of new business, but it made him a good sportsman.

Sir Thomas Lipton became known throughout the world as a good businessman, and as a famous yachtsman. Many times Americans and Englishmen cheered for him as his boat raced for the famous America's cup, the highest prize in yachting. He tried to win the cup five times, but he lost each time. Even though he never won, Sir Thomas was so greatly admired and respected for his fine sportsmanship, that he is still remembered. But very few people know the names of those who did win the cup.

More To Read

Let's Go Boating by Harry Zarchy. Published by Alfred A. Knopf, Inc., New York, 1952.

First Boat by Carroll B. Colby. Published by Coward-McCann, Inc., New York, 1956.

"WHAT'S THE MATTER WITH DIRT?"

BY RACHEL BARON

Jimmie stood at the edge of a busy street and counted the carriages going by. Each time he counted, he bounced his new red ball.

One-two-three, bounce-bounce-bounce.

The traffic was heavy. Sometimes three or four carriages would pass at once, and Jimmie would bounce his ball in rapid succession. He was a very good bouncer and hadn't missed a single carriage.

Jimmie decided to see how good his ball really was, how high it would bounce. So he threw it down hard on the ground and watched it bounce up over his head.

The boy reached out to catch the ball. But his foot slipped, and he lost his balance. He stumbled into the midst of the traffic, right in the path of an approaching cart.

Jimmie tried to jump aside. But he couldn't get out of the way in time. The cart came on, and its heavy, dirty wheels ran over the boy's left leg.

Jimmie lay without moving in the street. For a moment, he

could feel nothing. Everything began to turn dark except for streaks of yellow which flared in his head. Then his leg began to hurt.

"Help!" Jimmie cried. Tears welled in his eyes for he was in great pain. He tried to move, but he couldn't.

He was dimly aware of a crowd of men, women, and children that had gathered around him. Two gentlemen stepped forward and leaned over him. Then Jimmie's mother and father appeared.

Everybody stood close, and they made a lot of noise with their talking.

Jimmie's head was swimming. Jimmie's father stooped down and raised the boy in his arms. The boy, barely conscious, realized for the first time that his leg was bleeding. The blood ran down over his father's arm. Then Jimmie began to feel frightened. He buried his face in his father's shoulder.

"Here! Use this," called a friend who placed an old dirty rag from the gutter around Jimmie's open wound. "That'll slow down the bleeding."

"Get him to the infirmary!" shouted another.

The voices grew fainter and fainter. Jimmie slumped against his father's shoulder. Then he felt nothing.

When Jimmie opened his eyes again, he was lying in bed. He looked around. He was in a large room with many other sick people. He knew this must be the infirmary.

Jimmie took a deep breath. His head filled with a ghastly smell he had never known before. He closed his eyes. His pain was great and he tightened his fists.

He grabbed onto the bedclothes. Then he realized that his hands were empty. He wondered what had happened to his ball. And then he remembered the cart.

Jimmie heard the door to the corridor open. He opened his eyes wide. He saw a strange man enter the room and walk toward him.

"How do you do, Jimmie?" the man asked with a kindly voice. "Not so well, I dare say."

Jimmie wondered how the man knew his name. "Who—who are you?" he asked.

48

"Me? I'm nobody special, just the chief surgeon," the man answered. He placed his hand on Jimmie's leg.

"Ouch!" Jimmie cried.

The chief surgeon loosened the dirty cloth around the boy's wound and removed it slowly.

"Ooooooh, ooooooh," Jimmie yelled.

"Yell as loud as you like, my boy, if it makes you feel better. I know this hurts, but it has to be done. There, there, try to relax. You will feel better soon."

The chief surgeon took a sponge and washed off the sore. He looked hard at the wound, and the look on his face became very serious. Jimmie thought he saw the chief surgeon shake his head, ever so slightly.

"Am—am I going to be all right? Am I?" Jimmie asked fearfully.

The chief surgeon continued to examine the boy carefully. Every few seconds, he sponged Jimmie's wound.

"Am I going to get well?" Jimmie begged to know.

The chief surgeon looked hard at the boy's pleading face. "How old are you, Jimmie?" he asked.

"Eleven."

"Well, you are pretty grown-up then, aren't you?"

"Please, doctor, please tell me if I am going to be all right."

The chief surgeon rested his hand on Jimmie's shoulder. "You are a big boy, so I am going to be honest with you," he said. "We never know what will happen, especially with an open wound. There is always a danger that an open wound will cause hospital fever."

A fearful expression passed over Jimmie's face. He had often heard of hospital fever. Many people who were sent to hospitals developed this dreadful disease. As a result, many became crippled for life or even died from the smallest open sores.

The doctor began to talk again. "Jimmie, I am sure I can make your leg well. I have found a new medicine which I think will stop hospital fever. But you must help me. I am going to try the new medicine on you. Will you trust me?"

Jimmie still felt the pain in his leg, but he also felt a great relief. "Yes, doctor, I will trust you. I will," he said.

The chief surgeon disappeared for a few minutes. When he came back, he was with a second doctor who was carrying a piece of cloth and a bottle. The second doctor sat down on the chair next to Jimmie's bed. Then he pulled down the sheet that covered the boy's leg.

The second doctor tipped the bottle onto the cloth. A liquid ran out and soaked the pale-colored material.

Jimmie watched in fascination. "Is that the medicine?" he asked the chief surgeon.

"Yes, son. It is a chemical called carbolic acid. And you will be one of the first patients to use it."

The second doctor placed the moistened cloth on the boy's wound. He pressed down the edges until it was firmly set so no air could get through.

"What will the medicine do?" Jimmie asked.

"It will clean out all the dirt from your sore," the chief surgeon answered. "That filthy rag you were wearing when you came in must have filled your sore with many unclean particles."

The boy pondered a moment. Should he ask a question? He began slowly, "But what is the matter with dirt? I like to play in mud, especially after rain."

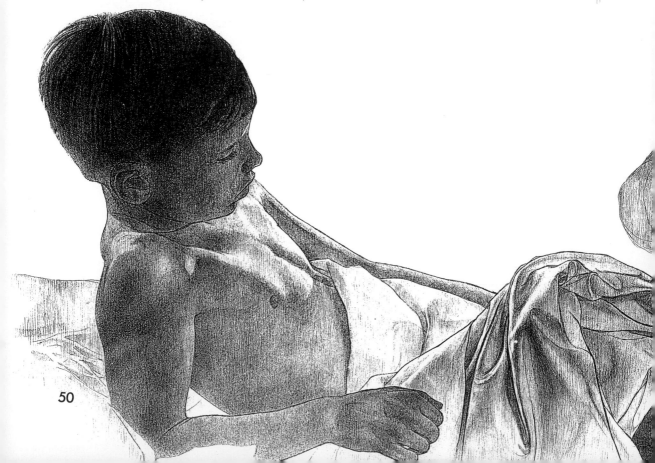

"Ah, yes, Jimmie, but you don't have open wounds when you play. I'll tell you a secret, my boy. There are many who might disagree with me. But I expect to save your leg by keeping the wound clean." The chief surgeon smiled and patted the boy's head. "Now, Jimmie, go to sleep if you can. There is nothing we can do now but wait."

Jimmie felt tired. He watched the chief surgeon and the second doctor walk out to the corridor. And then he fell asleep.

Every morning, the chief surgeon had come to see Jimmie. Today was the fourth day that Jimmie had been in the hospital.

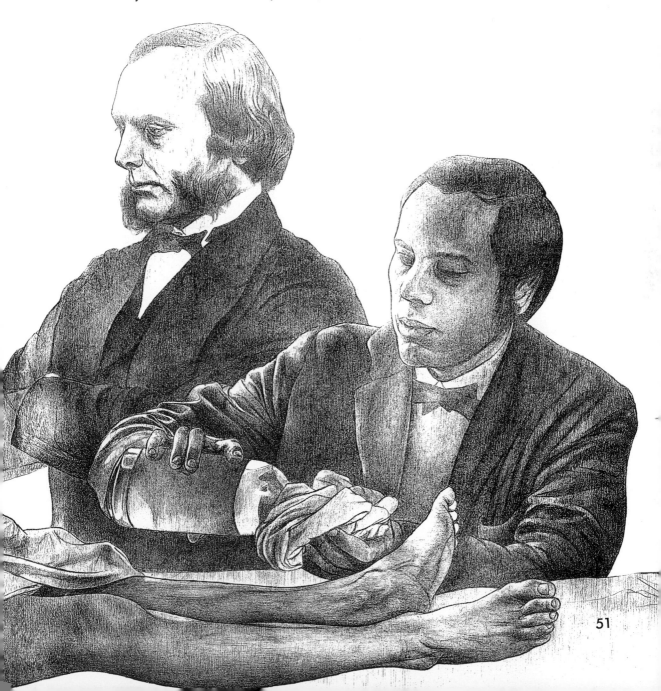

51

He sat up in bed waiting for the surgeon. His knee hurt badly.

Finally, the chief surgeon opened the door and came into the room. "Well, there, how are you today?" he asked.

Jimmie tried to smile but he couldn't. Instead his mouth twitched. He felt as if he were about to cry.

"Why, Jimmie, what is the matter?" the chief surgeon asked with a worried expression on his face.

"My leg hurts terribly this morning," Jimmie answered.

"Well, we'll see," replied the chief surgeon cautiously. "Tell me, how do you feel otherwise? Did you eat your breakfast this morning?"

"Oh yes, I ate everything the nurse brought me. Except— except . . ."

"Yes?"

"Well, there wasn't enough oatmeal."

The chief surgeon laughed. "Well, that's certainly a good sign," he said. "Now stick out your tongue and say Ah."

The doctor looked at Jimmie's tongue. Then he checked Jimmie's pulse and temperature.

"So far, you look just fine," he said. "Can you bend your knee so I can have a look at your sore?"

Jimmie winced as he bent his knee. It hurt terribly. Gently the chief surgeon removed the cloth and peered down at the sore. Then he blinked his eyes.

"What is it, doctor?" Jimmie cried. "Please tell me what's wrong."

"Nothing's wrong, Jimmie," the doctor answered with a kind smile. "I was just amazed at how well your wound has healed. There's no infection and you haven't a sign of hospital fever."

"But if my leg is well, why does it hurt?" Jimmie asked.

"The medicine I used cleaned your sore and helped your leg to heal. But it was too strong and it has irritated the skin around the sore. The pain will go away in just a few days, I'm sure. I have to put more medicine on your leg, but this time I won't make it so strong."

"Doctor, please don't weaken the medicine," Jimmie said. "My leg doesn't hurt that much. Make the medicine stronger. Make it as strong as you can so it will cure my leg for sure."

The chief surgeon patted the boy's shoulder. Then with a kind expression the chief surgeon said, "Jimmie, don't worry. I can weaken the chemical and it will still be strong enough to protect your wound. Your leg is going to be all right."

The chief surgeon in this story was Sir Joseph Lister. This story took place in Glasgow, Scotland, around the time of the American Civil War.

Before this story took place, half the people who were operated on died because doctors didn't realize that germs caused infection. Joseph Lister was the first to realize the danger of germs and dirt on an open wound. He called his method of cleaning wounds the Antiseptic Technique. This technique is practiced in all hospitals today. Since Sir Joseph Lister's discovery, the danger of a patient's dying from infection after an operation or because of an open sore is very slight.

Jimmie's leg did get better. Within a few weeks he was outdoors playing again as though nothing had ever happened to him.

Sir Joseph Lister

More To Read

The World of the Microscope by L. J. Ludovici. Published by G. P. Putnam's Sons, New York, 1959.

Courage of Dr. Lister by Iris Noble. Published by Julian Messner, New York, 1960.

Master Surgeon; a Biography of Joseph Lister by Laurence Farmer. Published by Harper & Row, New York, 1962.

CHAPPIE COULDN'T SMILE

By William Corbin

Joe, the heavyweight boxing champion of the world, sat on the rubbing table in his dressing room. His purple robe was draped across his powerful shoulders. His hands were taped, and the boxing gloves were laced tightly about his wrists. He was ready. But for the first time in his boxing career his usually calm, expressionless face wore a frown of worry, even of fear.

Joe had trained hard for this fight, as he always did. His opponent was Buddy Baer, the brother of Max Baer, the ex-heavyweight champ. Buddy Baer was big and dangerous. It was quite possible that this evening might end with Buddy Baer as heavyweight champion of the world.

But Joe wasn't even thinking about these things.

Worry and fear were in Joe's eyes because he had suddenly noticed something strange and disturbing about the slender little man who seemed to be huddling rather than sitting on a battered stool in front of him.

"Chappie!" Joe said. "What's wrong? You look sick!" The thought really frightened Joe because Jack Blackburn, whom he called "Chappie," was much more than a trainer and ring handler. He was in many ways more of a father than Joe's real father had been.

In every one of Joe's professional fights, little Jack Blackburn had been in Joe's corner, climbing up the steps to the ring at the end of each round and down again when the bell rang for the next. Jack's steady hands were always there to help when Joe was hurt. His wise advice was always in Joe's ear to tell him what he had done wrong in the last round and what he must do in the next.

It was because of Jack Blackburn that Joe leaned forward, suddenly tense, and repeated his question. "What's wrong, Chappie? You don't look good!"

Jack Blackburn tried to smile, but he couldn't. It was more a grimace of pain. He hugged his knees with his bony arms. "Just that old arthritis, boy," Jack said, stifling a gasp. "Don't you fret. It'll go away."

Joe slid off the rubbing table and stood towering above the little man. He felt cold with fear and as helpless as a baby. He wished that he knew what to do.

At that moment the door of the dressing room swung open and a man thrust his head in. "Okay, Joe. Time to go!"

Joe turned back to Jack. "You heard the man, Chappie," he said, trying to say it in a teasing way. "Come on!"

Slowly Jack looked up at him and shook his head. "Can't do it. Seems like I'm taken bad this time. I can't make it up and down those steps. I—I reckon this time, you got to go out there alone."

Joe heard the mumble of the crowd rise to a roar. Buddy Baer must be on his way to the ring. Joe bent down, put his big gloved hands under Chappie's elbows and raised him gently to his feet.

"You've *got* to come with me," he pleaded. It wasn't at all that Joe was afraid to go out there alone and fight Buddy Baer or any man living. Not that at all. But it just wouldn't be right. This was an important night for Joe, and Jack had to be there to share it with him. "I'll help you up the steps. I'll—" Joe stopped, struck by a sudden thought. The worry in his face turned to grim determination. "Chappie!" he burst out. "You know I'm no good without you. Will you come out there if I promise you that you'll only have to go up those steps to the ring *once?*"

Chappie looked up at Joe. The expression on his face told Joe that he knew what had been promised. Joe was determined to win the fight in a single round!

"Well, Chappie, how about it?" Joe asked. "Will you go up to the ring with me just once?"

Jack swung a feeble punch at Joe's strong jaw. "Okay," he said softly. "Let's get going."

In the glare of the ring lights, Joe stood quietly in his corner. The little man was there by his side.

The referee stepped to the center of the ring. He motioned to both fighters and Joe stepped forward, his face the expressionless mask so familiar to millions of boxing fans.

With a hand on the shoulder of each fighter, the referee recited the traditional instructions. Each man had heard them countless times. "No low blows . . . no hitting in the clinches . . . break clean . . . and may the best man win!"

Joe touched gloves with his towering opponent and trotted back to his corner. The voice of the crowd rose thunderously.

Joe took one more worried look at Chappie's thin, drawn face. The older man touched Joe gently on the arm. There was time for only a few words. "I won't hold you to your promise. You take care of yourself," Chappie said.

Then Chappie left the ring, crawling slowly and awkwardly through the ropes.

Only a second or two remained now before the opening bell. Slowly, without his even thinking about it, Joe's gloved hands came up into fighting position.

The crowd was hushed now, waiting.

CLANG! Joe sprang from his corner like a race horse at the starting gate.

Before the bell had even stopped echoing, he was throwing punches at Buddy Baer. The startled Baer met a hailstorm of rights and lefts to the head and body. He could only cover up and try to paw his way out of the storm with an uncertain left jab.

Baer took a stunning right to the chin but managed to throw an uppercut that caught Joe in the mouth, a blow that could have killed an ordinary man. In the next second Joe moved in and threw a right with every ounce of his two hundred pounds behind it. The ring quivered as Buddy Baer fell to the canvas.

As a clever fighter should, Baer raised himself to one knee and stayed there while the referee counted to nine. Joe waited in a neutral corner, as tense as a tightly coiled spring.

At the count of nine, Baer got to his feet. Joe leaped forward again. Buddy Baer went down the second time.

Again Joe waited, straining like a guard dog on a leash. Joe took no pleasure in hurting any man. But he was a professional boxer. And he was there to win. Joe knew the seconds were ticking by and that he had to finish this fight so Chappie wouldn't have to climb those steps again. He had to!

Baer was on his feet again.

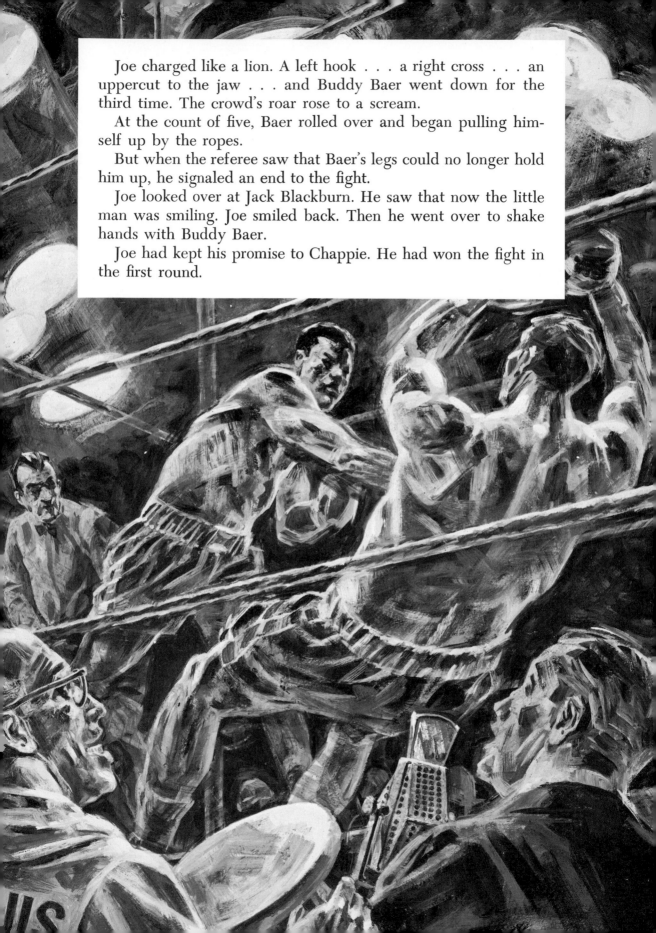

Joe charged like a lion. A left hook . . . a right cross . . . an uppercut to the jaw . . . and Buddy Baer went down for the third time. The crowd's roar rose to a scream.

At the count of five, Baer rolled over and began pulling himself up by the ropes.

But when the referee saw that Baer's legs could no longer hold him up, he signaled an end to the fight.

Joe looked over at Jack Blackburn. He saw that now the little man was smiling. Joe smiled back. Then he went over to shake hands with Buddy Baer.

Joe had kept his promise to Chappie. He had won the fight in the first round.

Joe in this story was Joe Louis Barrow, better known as Joe Louis, one of the greatest prize fighters the world has known. This story took place in New York's Madison Square Garden, in 1942, just after the start of World War II.

Shortly after Joe defeated Buddy Baer, he hung up his gloves and put on a new uniform—the uniform of the United States Army. During the war Joe served his country with the same honor and determination that he had always shown in the boxing ring.

After the war Joe went back to boxing. He held the world's heavyweight championship for a total of twelve years. Finally, in 1949, he retired from the ring. Later he tried to make two comebacks, but both attempts failed.

Joe Louis defended his championship twenty-five times. He won each of these fights. But one of his most memorable victories took place on the night he kept his promise to little Jack Blackburn.

More To Read

Better Boxing for Boys by George Sullivan. Published by Dodd, Mead & Company, New York, 1966.

Joe Louis defeats Max Baer, Buddy Baer's brother, in 1935.

"Slide, Connie, Slide!"

By Marcella Rawe

A tall, thin boy came up the back walk slowly, carrying his empty lunch bucket. He wiped his feet and closed the screen door behind him without slamming it. He had something to tell his mother. But he didn't know how to say it.

As usual, the kitchen was busy and noisy. Ma was bending over the stove dishing up supper. And sister Nellie was carefully placing the hot platters of food on the red-checkered cloth that covered the kitchen table.

"Is that you, Connie?" called ma over her shoulder. "Hurry and wash up. Supper is ready."

Connie washed quickly and took his place among his brothers and sisters. Everyone muttered a short grace, and then Pa began filling the plates.

Supper in the McGillicuddy household was always a pleasant time. Pa and brother Michael shared jokes with the family. Something funny was always happening at the wagon factory where they both worked. Ma listened and laughed like one of the children. But tonight Connie, usually the gayest at the table, was quiet and thoughtful.

"Eat your meal, Connie," ma said. "What's ailing you, lad?"

Connie swallowed a few bites. What can I say to her? he thought. How can I make her understand?

When supper was over Connie did his nightly chore, filling the woodbox beside the big black stove. Then he went to sit alone on the back steps. His mother found him there, his long, skinny arms wrapped around his bony knees, his blue eyes fixed on the evening sky above the factory chimneys of the town.

"Now then, lad," she said, sitting down beside him. "Out with it. What's bothering you?"

"And what should be bothering me?" he asked, still not sure how to begin.

"When a gay lad acts like a wet cat in a fog, he's either got a pain in his stomach or something on his mind. So now, which is it?"

Connie drew a deep breath. "Well, ma, the boys at the factory have started a baseball team. They want me to play with them, and I want to play, ma. I want to play very much."

"Baseball, is it!"

Connie's heart fell at the tone of his mother's voice. "It's a wonderful game, ma," he said. "It really is!"

"Wonderful!" said ma coldly. "Wonderful for wearing out the knees of your pants sliding in the dirt!" She put her arm lovingly around Connie's thin shoulders. "I know you don't have much time for fun, working in that factory all summer long. And I don't mind you playing. But I can't see why batting a wee ball with a club is so important to you."

"Ma," Connie spoke very seriously. "It's so important that, if I can, I want to play professional baseball when I grow up."

"Oh, no, Connie!" cried his mother. "Most of the folks who play baseball for a living are a bad lot. You've been brought up to be a clean, decent lad. Baseball is not for the likes of you."

"All baseball players aren't bad, ma. A few bad ones have given the game a bad name. I wouldn't be like them," Connie said. "If you could see a good game of baseball you would understand why I love it. Wouldn't you come tomorrow evening and watch us?"

"I'll make no promises," ma said.

"Please, ma! If you don't *know* about something, how can you say if it's good or bad?" Connie pleaded.

"True enough," said his mother. She thought about it for a moment.

"I'll come," she decided, and went back into the house.

When the factory whistles blew at half past six the following evening, there were not so many workers going home as usual. Many stayed to watch the team play baseball. The team had no uniforms, so each of the boys wore a red handkerchief on his left arm. No one thought of wearing gloves. The catchers wore no masks or shin guards.

Connie tied his red handkerchief over his shirt sleeve and helped his teammates mark out the field. The playing field was backed by brick warehouse walls. It had bumps and hollows which sent a bouncing ball in any direction and sometimes caused runners to trip. But that was a part of the game.

As Connie worked, he kept watching the rickety little bleachers filling up rapidly with noisy fans. Would his mother really come?

Soon the opposing team rode up in a horse and wagon. They tied their horse behind the bleachers and ran across to their side of the field. They had gray uniforms with big letters on the fronts. Connie and his teammates admired those uniforms.

Crouching at home plate as he helped to "warm up" the pitcher, Connie kept watching for his mother. She had promised to come and she believed in keeping promises. Still there were many reasons why she might not be able to spend the supper hour watching her son bat a "wee ball with a club." Anxious as he was, Connie laughed to himself as he thought of his mother's words.

Just as he stood waiting his first turn at bat he saw her. She was standing near the bleachers looking for him. When she saw where he was standing, she sat down, holding her open black umbrella as a shield against curious faces and wild balls.

Connie strode to the batter's box waggling the bat in front of his shoulder. I've got to do well, he thought. I've got to show ma what a wonderful game—

"Stah-rike one!" cried the umpire. Connie stopped thinking of what he had to do and started to do it.

"Ball one," called the umpire.

Then, "Stah-rike two!"

This is it! thought Connie. He connected with the next pitch. It was a satisfying *whack!* With his long stride he got to second base while the fielders were still scurrying after the ball.

"That's the way, Slats!" yelled the fans. "Slats" was the nickname the people at the factory had given to Connie.

Connie looked across at ma. He was too far away to see the look on her face, but she had lowered her umbrella and was sitting alertly, following every play. Connie made it only to third base that inning, but the batter just ahead of him had scored because of his hit.

The score crept up inning by inning and the fans grew more and more excited. Connie glanced sideways at ma every little while. She was watching everything that went on very seriously. I've got to do well, Connie thought. I've got to do well in this game.

Slowly Connie's team began to pull ahead. In the ninth inning the score was twelve to eight in their favor. Then the other team got lucky. When Connie's team came to bat in their half of the ninth inning, the boys on the other team had tied the score.

Connie was next up to bat for his team. He really *did* have a chance to win the game now, but suddenly, there was a sinking feeling in his stomach. He wasn't a strong hitter, and a home run was what his team needed right now.

He picked up the bat as the fans yelled, "Come on, Slats! Hit a home run, Slats!"

He saw the ball coming and hit the first pitch.

Wham! The ball sliced off to the right. Connie ran like a scared rabbit.

The ball rolled past the first baseman's fingers. While the fielder fumbled for the ball, Connie streaked for second base. Fast as he was, he wouldn't have made it if the ball which the fielder threw hadn't hit a bump in the field.

Connie sped on to third base and started toward home plate. Lurching behind him, the third baseman caught the ball and threw it to the catcher. The ball sped along the line like a bee chasing a greyhound.

Through the noise of the crowd, Connie heard his mother's voice, **"Slide, Connie, Slide!"**

Connie threw his legs forward and slid home just ahead of the ball.

Picking himself up he saw ma keeping time with her umbrella as the fans yelled, **"Slats McGillicuddy! Slats McGillicuddy!"**

A few minutes later, with the game won thirteen to twelve, ma reached up to wipe a streak of dirt from Connie's chin, ignoring the rip in his shirt and the hole in his trousers.

"One thing, Connie," she said. "When you're a professional ballplayer you must tell folks to call you 'Cornelius' and not 'Slats.'"

"I'll tell them, ma," answered Connie with a grin.

They didn't call him Cornelius. They called him Connie Mack. But his real name was Cornelius McGillicuddy.

Connie did become a professional baseball player. And he later became one of the greatest baseball managers the game has known.

This story took place when baseball was still a new game. This is one of the stories Connie's friends and teammates liked to tell about him. In those days baseball was a rough game, and many of the players were rough characters. Connie Mack helped make baseball a clean and honorable game. He was one of the founders of the American League. He owned and managed the Philadelphia Athletics, now the Oakland Athletics, for fifty years. Under Connie's leadership, the Athletics won the American League pennant nine times, and the World Series five times. Connie managed the team until he was almost ninety years old.

Connie Mack's name is in the Baseball Hall of Fame in Cooperstown, New York, and in the hearts of baseball fans all over the world.

More To Read

Inside Big League Baseball by Roger Kahn. Published by The Macmillan Company, New York, 1962.

Connie Mack:
Manager of the Philadelphia Athletics
at the age of eighty-seven

By Mea Underwood

Alexander slammed the door shut and shouted, "Pierre, Pierre!"

Pierre, the boatman, came running around the side of the shed. Seeing Alexander's determined look, he stopped short.

"Pierre, we're going down the river to visit the Indian camps," Alexander announced. "I'm going to find out for myself what has happened to the fur pelts the Indians promised to bring us. We have nothing to show for our work but an empty shed."

Pierre nodded gravely. He knew that inside the shed, there were only a few piles of goods remaining from the great supply that they had carried with them into the wilderness. All the blankets, kettles, knives, mirrors, and tobacco had been given to the Indians. In return, the Indians had promised that when fall came to the Canadian wilderness, they would bring pelts of fur. But fall had come and gone, and there was no sign of the Indians or their furs.

Everyone in the little fort wondered why the Indians had broken their promise.

"Perhaps they have already traded their furs to someone else," said Pierre.

Alexander scowled, "If they have, we will fight them. They made a promise, and it's up to us to see that they keep it."

"But the river is nearly frozen," argued Pierre.

Alexander looked toward the river. Pierre was right. Frost bent the boughs of the willows along the shore. Thick ice covered the banks. And as the two men watched, blocks of ice crashed from the banks and were carried down the river by the swift current.

"It won't be easy," Alexander said. "But if we leave at once, we should be able to make the trip. Next week will be too late. By then the river will be covered with ice, and we will be stranded here all winter."

"Yes, you are right," Pierre answered. "We must go now."

"I want one of the small canoes," Alexander told Pierre. "We need to move as quickly as possible."

"I will get it ready," Pierre answered.

An hour later Alexander came down to the water's edge. He was bundled in his heavy coat.

Alexander stepped into the front of the canoe, Pierre into the back. They eased the canoe into the center of the river. The current began to carry them downstream. Mighty chunks of ice, broken away from the shore, swept around them. The river roared.

Alexander looked around at Pierre's grave face.

"Very bad!" Pierre shouted above the noise of the water.

"If we are careful, we can do it," Alexander called back.

He was pleased to see Pierre nod in agreement. But there was no time for talking. If the racing ice blocks struck their canoe, it would be smashed and their chances for swimming to safety would be slim indeed.

Alexander watched the rushing water like a hawk. His eyes darted back and forth, watching, watching.

The canoe raced along, swaying in the wake of the drifting ice. They were making good progress. They would soon be ap-

proaching the first Indian camp. It would not be long before they would know exactly what had become of their furs.

Alexander glanced toward the riverbank. A huge ice block had broken off the bank and was being swept midstream. At first it did not seem any different from the others. But when he looked a second time, he realized with horror that they were directly in its path. It was moving toward them with such speed that he could see no way to dodge it.

Alexander gave a shout of warning to Pierre.

But Pierre held his paddle above the water. He was paralyzed with fear.

"Pierre!" Alexander shouted again, his own paddle cutting the gray water with frantic strokes.

The shout brought Pierre back to his senses. In an instant he had thrust his paddle into the water. With all his great strength,

Pierre struggled to steer the canoe out of the path of the ice block.

The canoe swerved so suddenly that Alexander lost his balance and nearly toppled into the icy river. He kept paddling fiercely, expecting the tiny canoe to be smashed to bits at any moment.

But the collision didn't come! Was it possible that the ice block had missed the canoe?

Alexander did not dare look. Every muscle was strained to the limit with the effort of paddling.

But, finally, he glanced behind him. Out of the corner of his eye, he saw that the ice block had just barely missed the back of the canoe. The canoe began to bob crazily. They must keep it afloat!

Then, suddenly, they were safe, racing down the river, leaving the ice block behind.

"That was close!" shouted Pierre.

Alexander had no time to answer. Before them, the crude log huts of the Indian camp swept into view.

The two tired men paddled the canoe toward the camp. As soon as they reached the shore, Alexander leaped from the canoe and started to march toward the log huts.

Two Indians hurried toward him. As Alexander tramped along, he saw other Indians coming out of the huts. He could tell that they were excited.

In a moment Alexander was surrounded by Indians. He stood firm and unafraid.

The leader of the group was a tall, fierce-looking Indian. He motioned his people to stop chattering. A moment passed before the Indian spoke.

"Does the white man want the fur pelts my people have worked so hard to trap?" he finally asked.

Alexander was stunned. But quickly he replied, "Yes, of course! Why have you not brought them to me?"

There was another long silence, and then the Indian began to chuckle. Laughter started on the outskirts of the group and spread rapidly among the braves. Even the squaws began to snicker. Children rolled in merriment on the snow.

Alexander thought that they must all have gone crazy. What could possibly have been so funny?

Finally the Indian leader spoke up, "We thought you would come for the fur pelts. You thought we would bring them to you. So we both sat and wondered and wondered, and waited and waited, and no one did anything."

So that had been the trouble! The Indians had not broken their promise after all. Alexander tilted his head back and joined in the laughter.

"Come," the tall Indian said. "We wish to show you the pelts we have stored for you. They are many and beautiful."

Alexander Mackenzie, the young man in this story, was a well-known Canadian trader, explorer, and author. This incident happened nearly two hundred years ago in the wilderness of the Canadian Northwest.

In his trips through the wilderness, Alexander discovered many things about the Indians of Canada.

In 1793, he became the first man to cross the northern part of Canada and reach the Pacific Ocean.

After his many years of exploration, Alexander Mackenzie wrote books about his exciting adventures.

More To Read

Alexander Mackenzie, Canadian Explorer by Ronald Syme. Published by William Morrow & Co., Inc., New York, 1964.

Sir Alexander Mackenzie

The Swamp Fox's Secret Mission

By Dorfay

The general better known as "the Swamp Fox" read the last line of the message once more: "The mission must be secret to all except the generals."

He held the message to the open fire and watched it burn. Then he called for the drummer.

"Boy, how are your hands?" he asked.

A broad smile spread over the drummer's face. "Shall I roll the sticks? Do we march?"

The Swamp Fox stepped over to the youth and gave him a friendly slap on the shoulder. "We march."

"Booom-di-de-dum . . ." The drum sounded as if it were alive. At first, the boy beat the drum gently. As he became excited, he rolled the sticks faster and faster.

The small band of men gathered around with an eagerness that cheered the general.

"We have rested long enough, men," he said. "We have new orders. It's time to hit out against the Redcoats again." But the general did not mention what the orders were or to where they would be marching.

All day they moved south, through rice fields, through sand-beds, back into open fields, and finally into a thick pine forest. There they met Colonel Light-Horse Harry Lee with his legion of men. They had been ordered to join the general. The general gave the order to set up camp.

"Pitch the tents and we'll have a good night's sleep before we meet the Redcoats." The general walked through camp. He spoke warmly to the men.

"Well, now, you'd better put a patch in that boot, boy," he said to one soldier.

"Your horse needs a good combing, son," he advised another.

Then he gave words of encouragement to the men cleaning their muskets. "That's the way, lads. Keep your firing pieces sharp—you're about to get a chance to show your ability."

The Swamp Fox's men knew that they must be going into the thick of battle in the morning. The general always spent the night before a battle with them. They wondered where they would be going—what battle they would fight.

The men were awake before dawn. They broke camp and waited for orders.

"On to Nelson's Ferry," the general's voice rang out.

By nightfall they had passed Nelson's Ferry and reached Fort Watson, a major British stronghold.

Now the men knew the secret. They were to capture Fort Watson and cut off the British communications. There would be some real fighting now.

"Pitch the tents among the hawthorn trees, out of range of the fort," the general ordered.

"Lee, have your men fire at the fort. That will give me an idea of how strong they are."

A volley of shot from Lee's riflemen brought musket and cannon fire in return. The general knew this would not be a quick battle. The fort was a well-constructed log stockade with cannons and much ammunition. Without cannons the Americans could not outfire the British. The Swamp Fox would have to outwit them.

"Sarg," he called to one of his trusted marksmen. "Take some men over by that lake. It is out of range of the fort so you won't need much cover. And don't let a single Redcoat take a drop of water!"

The Swamp Fox smiled and chuckled to himself as he turned to Light-Horse Harry. "This may not be as bad as we thought. We can just sit here and take it easy till they get thirsty!"

There was merriment in the general's camp that night and during the day that followed. Now it seemed to be just a waiting game. Occasionally there would be the whine of a rifle shot as someone attempted to run from the fort to the lake. The only other sounds were those made by the men tending to the ordinary tasks of camp life.

Then another sound came from inside the fort. There was a hush in the American camp as they listened.

"What can they be doing?" Lee asked the general.

"I don't know—" the general started to say. Then he recognized the sound. It was the sound of digging. "They outfoxed me!" he groaned. "They are digging a well!"

"Now what do we do?"

"I don't know," replied the general. "Their cannons are too powerful for us. We can't move any closer to the fort."

Every muscle in his face was tight as he thrust his hands deep into his pockets and paced around the tents. The men dared not speak to him. They had seen their leader deep in thought before.

The Swamp Fox knew there must be a way to defeat the British commander. Maybe one of the men would have an idea. He stopped and asked one and then another what he thought they could do. The general considered each suggestion, but went on pacing and thinking.

Then Major Hezekiah Maham had an idea. The general listened with interest to the major's plan. A twinkle came into his eyes. He straightened his back, smiled, and took a deep breath before he gave the order, "Lee, have a squadron go to the plantations in the area and get all the axes they can lay their hands on! If the Redcoats can build, so can we!"

Excitement spread through the camp when the men saw the change in the Swamp Fox.

"The 'Fox' is at it again!" they whispered.

They had no idea what they would build, but whatever it was, they were ready to build it.

When the men returned with the axes, the general called Major Maham. "Major," he said, "this is your idea. Take as many men as you need. Build me a tower to beat all towers."

A tower! The word spread quickly among the men.

Work started immediately. Major Maham sent men to chop down trees. He sent others to gather ropes and leather straps. Holes were dug to give a good foundation to the tower. The men laughed when they saw the British looking over the walls of the fort at them.

"Just wait," they yelled. "We'll show you!" Though truly they were not sure what they would show them.

For hours the sound of splitting logs filled the woods. The men worked quickly, eager to find out what the secret plan would be.

Finally, the tower reached the desired height. The men reinforced the front of the tower with a solid wall of timber. While they were tying in the last logs, the general was already at work preparing for the maneuver that would follow.

He called to his best riflemen, "All right, men. When you climb onto that tower, you will be able to see every nook and cranny in the whole fort!"

A whoop and yell went through the American camp. Now they would be able to fight as if there were no fort at all. They

would have more protection than those in the fort. Their rifles had longer range than the British muskets, and the buckshot from the muskets could not pierce the shield of logs.

The general's men climbed the tower and the firing began. Shots rained into the fort.

The British troops crouched in the shadows of the high wall facing the tower. That was the only safe spot.

But there was no way for them to escape or shoot back.

When the general saw that they were safe, he sent several of his men with axes to the wall of the fort. With the bullets of their own men whining above their heads, they chopped away at the wall. The British could do nothing. They continued to hide behind the wall.

Soon the Americans had chopped their way through. The British stood helpless before them. The battle was over!

Shouts of joy went through the American camp as they saw a white flag hoisted over Fort Watson. The British had surrendered. The mission was completed.

"Roll that drum, boy," the soldiers called out. "The Swamp Fox has done it again!"

The general called "the Swamp Fox" was General Francis Marion. He was named "the Swamp Fox" because of his daring raids. He and his men would dart out of the marshes to strike a severe blow against the British, and then vanish into the swamps again. The Swamp Fox was loved and admired by his men because of his daring and bravery and because of the fair way he treated them.

The surrender of Fort Watson, a vital British fort in South Carolina, was an important victory for the Americans during the Revolutionary War. It cut off communications between the two main British headquarters in Camden and Charleston, South Carolina, and helped turn the tide of battle in the southern colonies toward the American forces.

South Carolina Swampland

More To Read

Swamp Fox of the Revolution by Stewart Holbrook. Published by Random House, New York, 1959.

The Swamp Fox by Marion Marsh Brown. Published by The Westminster Press, Philadelphia, 1950.

"I CAN DO IT!"

By Thelma Wilson

Bob sat outside in the warm sunshine and watched his older brother Gene get ready for a hike in the woods. Bob wanted so much to go along but he had been sick with anemia, an illness that makes people weak. Now he had to take things easy until he was stronger. Gene was always hiking and playing games with his friends while Bob just had to stay quiet and watch them.

Gene glanced up just as a big tear slid down Bob's cheek. Bob sniffed and wiped his face on his sleeve.

Nuts! he thought. Now Gene has seen me acting like a baby.

But Gene pretended not to notice. "Hey Sprout, how would you like to go with me today?" he asked. "I'm going to hunt for some more bird eggs for my collection. I'll run in and ask Mom if it will be all right for you to come along."

Joy flooded Bob's face like sunshine after a shower. "Gee, that would be great!" he said as Gene walked into the house.

Gene returned a few minutes later. "Mom says it will be okay if you promise to take it easy," Gene told him.

"Can I really go?" Bob asked, not quite believing that he had heard right.

"Sure, Sprout. But—may I, not can I."

"Yeah—may I? Oh, boy! I won't run—or get too tired—or nothing."

"Or ANYTHING, Bob. Jeepers, where do you pick up your English? Well, get your boots. Mom's packing our lunch."

As they started off, their mother called from the kitchen door. "Now Gene . . . I'm trusting you to be sure your brother doesn't get too tired. And he's not to run, or climb too high."

"Sure, Mom!" Gene called.

By noon the boys were high on a sunny ridge, munching peanutbutter sandwiches and apples. Suddenly, Gene whispered, "Look—up there—way up in that big pine. A red-shouldered hawk! Boy, oh boy! I've been looking for hawk eggs for two years."

Lunch was forgotten as the brothers scrambled to reach the big tree. But when they got there Gene's grin vanished. The lowest branch was more than three feet above his upstretched arms.

Bob jumped up and down with excitement. "Gene! I can do it. Hoist me up so I can grab that branch and I'll see if there are any eggs in the nest."

Gene looked up the towering tree. "I don't know, Sprout. Mom would skin me alive if you got hurt."

For a minute Bob studied the tree. Then he looked straight into his brother's eyes and said quietly, "Gene, I can do it!"

His big brother smiled to hear those familiar words. Ever since Bob had learned to talk those words had been his motto.

"Okay!" Gene agreed. "Up you go . . . but be careful."

Slowly Bob worked his way up the tree, stretching from branch to branch.

Suddenly, the hawk screeched, and with a flash of speckled wings, flew from the nest.

Bob climbed higher and higher until he finally reached the nest.

"Hey Gene! Gene, I made it! There are four eggs here—beauties!"

"Just take two," Gene shouted. "Now listen! Don't put them in your pocket. They'll get smashed. Put them in your mouth,

one in each cheek, like a squirrel. Understand?"

Bob nodded his head, and put the eggs in his mouth.

"Now, come down slowly. SLOWLY, Sprout," Gene called.

Nervously Bob inched his way down from the swaying branch, stretching for a toe-hold as his arms strained to hang on.

"Bob! SLOW DOWN! Easy does it," Gene warned.

Bob was tired now, his hands were slick with perspiration. He couldn't breathe very well with his mouth closed firmly over the two eggs. He looked down, his lungs aching for more air. He had about twelve more feet to go.

"Shinny down," Gene yelled. "I'll help you."

Bob shook his head, flexed his knees, let go, and crashed with a heavy thump . . . right on a soft bed of pine needles beneath the tree. As he rolled over, unhurt, a look of astonishment covered his face. His mouth dropped open.

Out peeked a tiny bird's head . . . then another!

The eggs had hatched on the trip down!

"Cheep! Cheep! Cheep!" chirped the birds.

Bob sat there holding the baby hawks in one hand and spitting egg shells while his brother howled with laughter.

"That's the funniest sight I ever saw in my whole life," he gasped. "You hatched them . . . your name is now Mama Bird!"

"Cut it out," Bob grinned foolishly. "I probably cracked the shells when I landed. Just the same . . . I said I could do it, and I did."

Bob, the young "Mama Bird" in this story, was Robert Bruce Mathias, a great athlete and Olympic champion.

This story took place in California when Bob Mathias was twelve years old.

His motto of "I can do it" led Bob Mathias to great victories in both the 1948 and 1952 Olympic games. In both these years he won the hardest contest in the Olympics, the decathlon, in which an athlete must compete in ten events. This meant that he was the best all-around athlete in the Olympics. At seventeen he was the youngest athlete ever to win the decathlon.

Bob Mathias competing in the broad jump during the 1952 Olympic games

More To Read

Highlights of the Olympics, From Ancient Times to the Present by John Durant. Published by Hastings House, Publishers, Inc., New York, 1961.

Young Olympic Champions by Steve Gelman. Published by W. W. Norton & Company, Inc., New York, 1964.

Sitting Bull Meets His Match

by T. Morris Longstreth

Young Constable Jack Lane turned his horse again. He was riding herd on forty Mounted Police horses while they grazed. He looked across the riverbed at the Indian camp. Hundreds of Sitting Bull's Indians were camped there. Trouble could break out at any minute, and there were thirty Sioux warriors to every Mountie at the fort. It was indeed a dangerous situation.

It's lucky that Inspector Allen is in command, Lane thought.

Distant hoofbeats directed Lane's gaze toward the clustered tepees. A dozen of Sitting Bull's young braves were nearing some straying horses. Lane galloped toward the Indians, shouting as he rode. But they had already cut four horses out of the herd and were driving them toward their camp.

Lane reached for his rifle. Despite years of danger, the Mounted Police had never killed an Indian. Lane was not going to spoil that record now. He shot over the heads of the racing redskins. But they kept going, and he turned back sadly. He had let Inspector Allen down.

Soon the man who was to relieve him rode up from the fort, and Lane went to report the stolen horses to Inspector Allen.

Inspector Allen looked up from his desk as Lane strode into his office. The Inspector listened to Lane's report without comment. When Lane had finished speaking, Allen said, "You did what you could. Now we will do more."

He called out eight of his staunchest men. Constable Lane was proud to be included. He felt responsible for letting the horses get away and wanted to help get them back.

As the Mounties rode toward the Sioux camp at a brisk trot, Inspector Allen said, "Look bold, men. Sitting Bull knows he is an intruder here. He knows we can drive his six thousand Sioux out of Canada. Whatever my commands are, obey them at once and without question."

Inspector Allen's self-confidence made Constable Lane feel sure of himself. He glanced at the rest of the Mounties. They looked imposing and stern.

They neared the Sioux camp. Angry braves galloped their ponies in a wide circle around Sitting Bull's tepee. The bodies of the young braves were painted with red and yellow stripes. Their shrill cries mixed with the screeches of the angry squaws.

Inspector Allen led his men straight into the camp as if nothing were in his way. Constable Lane tried not to show his worry. The painted braves made no attempt to stop the Mounties, but the ring of Indians closed behind them, cutting off any escape. Jack Lane knew that one wrong move could bring death to all.

In his two years among these Indians, Lane had learned enough of the Sioux language to act as an interpreter. Inspector Allen called Lane up to ride beside him. Sitting Bull was awaiting them on a horse outside his tepee.

"The nerve of him!" Allen exclaimed. "That's one of our horses."

Sitting Bull's long black hair hung down to his shoulders. His eyes darted from side to side. His high cheekbones, big nose, heavy jaw, and broad forehead made him look powerful. He waited for the Inspector to speak.

"Your young men have taken horses belonging to our Queen, whom you call White Mother," Allen said, and Lane repeated in the Sioux language. "We want them back. We want you to punish those who took our horses."

"I am tired of so much fuss over a few horses," Sitting Bull said. "They might as well remain where they are."

"You had best remember where *you* are!" Allen snapped back.

Lane tried to put the Inspector's force into the softer Indian words.

"Have you forgotten you are guests of Canada?" Allen asked. "The White Mother is tired of the trouble you cause her police. You steal horses. You kill buffalo. I order you to send four men to bring me the horses."

The expression on Sitting Bull's face never changed, but the glitter in his eyes showed his raging anger. "Be careful!" he said. "You speak to the head of the Sioux nation."

Allen urged his horse closer to the huge Indian. "You think all white men are afraid of you. You are wrong. When you stay here in Canada, you must obey the laws of the White Mother. Send the men for our horses *now!*"

Sitting Bull's temper was now at its ugliest. "The men would like to see you try to take the horses."

This was bluffing indeed, thought Lane. What would Allen say now?

The Inspector had moved his horse to within inches of Sitting Bull's. "Hand over our horses at once, or the White Mother will send you back to the United States. Our law says you must not steal. If that horse you ride was stolen, I will have to take it."

Lane gasped.

Sitting Bull's eyes shone with a wild light as he said, "It is stolen."

Lane sat frozen in the saddle. How could Inspector Allen make good on this impossible threat? The Inspector was leaning forward. Swiftly he threw his right arm about Sitting Bull's body. He lifted Sitting Bull from the saddle with one gigantic heave and dropped him down to the ground. Then he seized the horse's bridle, wheeled, and ordered his men to follow.

It all happened in less than a second. But it was an act of such power and daring that it surprised the Indians just long enough to give the Mounties a chance to start away. Lane rode close to Inspector Allen, keeping the recovered horse between them. The others formed a circle around them.

Then came the Indians.

The bareback Indian riders charged in on the Mounties. They reached for Allen's horse and had their arms knocked back. They tried to trip up the trained Mounted Police horses with rawhide ropes, but the Mounties pressed on. The painted Indians, screeching and whirling tomahawks, got in one another's way. No shot was fired, no tomahawk was flung. The braves could not stop the Mounties. They began dropping back until only one brave still followed.

"I must speak to him," Lane said to Allen. "He is my friend,

Gray Horn."

"Take care," Allen shouted as Lane dropped back.

Gray Horn, swinging his tomahawk as if to smash Lane's skull, glided past the young constable. He whispered something in Lane's ear as he passed. Lane rejoined his comrades at a gallop. Allen said, "I thought he was going to take your scalp and your head with it."

"No fear. We are blood brothers," Lane said. "He told me that we would be attacked by daybreak."

They rode in silence back to the fort.

The night was filled with a strange quiet as the Mounties waited for morning.

As dawn came, the unusual lull ended. A fierce war whoop split the air outside the fort.

The sentry at the gate ran to Inspector Allen. "Sitting Bull wishes to speak with you, sir."

"It's about time!" Allen said coolly. "Let him in! Then bar the gate behind him. Tell him I guarantee his safety on the word of the White Mother."

Allen turned to his men. "Place the muzzles of your rifles in

the holes drilled in the walls of the barracks, but don't let them be seen. I shall stand by the storehouse door. If I raise one hand and wave it around, push the muzzles out. If I raise my gun, shoot to kill."

He said to Lane, "Stand beside me to interpret."

That was Lane's grandest moment. Lane, who was as tall as Inspector Allen, kept step with him, proud of his uniform, and glad of his usefulness.

Sitting Bull approached on horseback. He rode proudly and seemed not to hear the gate shut behind him.

Without speaking of the stolen horses, Sitting Bull said, "Our stomachs are empty. We want to fill them."

"You should have thought of that last night," Allen instructed Lane to tell Sitting Bull. "I have no food for you."

"I can summon more warriors than there are blades of grass in this field."

"I, too, have fighters," Allen snapped.

"My squaws are hungry. The buffalo are gone," Sitting Bull said. "My young men cannot become strong without food."

"Go to the trading post. They will give you rations."

"They give little. Here there is food for my people. My young men will not wait. They will take."

To Lane's surprise, Allen said, "All right. Try and get food if you can. I will open the gates. *But you will pay.* Be sure of that."

Sitting Bull pretended not to hear this warning. He wheeled his pony and started back. Allen shouted to the sentry to open the gates. A crowd of young braves pushed into the square, eager to loot the fort. They saw an empty square and two Mounties standing in front of the door of the house that held stores of food and ammunition.

So still, so erect and forbidding stood the officer and the constable that it threw a doubt into the minds of the Indians. The Mounties did not look frightened. They made no friendly gestures. Something was wrong here. Something was very wrong. Could it be a trap?

The braves stopped, stared, began to mumble. Without warning or sound, Allen raised one hand and waved it at the barracks on three sides of the square. The Indians followed his gesture and their mumbling grew louder. They saw rifle muzzles pop through the holes.

Panic seized the braves. One turned and ran. The others wavered and then followed. They scattered in massed confusion with Sitting Bull lost among them. In minutes the square was emptied. The sentry barred the gates.

The Mounties had lost three horses. But Lane knew that Sitting Bull would steal no more.

Inspector Allen turned to Constable Lane and said, "It pays to stand your ground—if you are right."

Lane nodded and swallowed hard. It would not do for him to show that anything unusual had taken place.

Inspector Edwin Allen and Constable Jack Lane were among the first to wear the uniform of the North-West Mounted Police, later known as the Royal Canadian Mounted Police. This story took place in 1878, just five years after the Mounted Police had been established. The problem they faced with Sitting Bull was one of the first problems the Mounties had to solve. In 1881, Sitting Bull led his Sioux followers back to the United States and finally to a reservation in South Dakota.

The courage and daring shown by Lane and Allen have remained a tradition of the Mounted Police.

The Mounties were organized to bring law and order to the unsettled territory of the Canadian Northwest. They helped the friendly Indians and tried to keep the unfriendly ones from causing trouble. They made it possible for peace-loving people to settle in the Northwest.

Today the Mounties have many more duties than they had in 1878. They carry the mails to distant settlements, fight forest fires, and care for the sick. But their main duty, still, is to maintain law and order. There is a saying in Canada that a Mountie always gets his man. And the truth is that few criminals escape when the Royal Canadian Mounted Police are on their trail.

More To Read

The Sioux Indians: Hunters and Warriors of the Plains by Sonia Bleeker. Published by William Morrow & Co., Inc., New York, 1962.

Royal Canadian Mounted Police by Richard Lewis Neuberger. Published by Random House, New York, 1953.

The Order

By Mary-Anne Amsbary

of the Golden Spur

"Do you admit that you were in the Sistine Chapel last Wednesday?"

The thirteen-year-old boy looked up into the face of the fierce soldier. He was too frightened to answer.

"Yes, sir, we were there," said the boy's father. "But we took nothing."

The soldier strode across the small room, straight to the writing desk. The tall plumes on his great metal helmet shook, and his huge sword clanked. On the desk were scattered many sheets of music paper. The soldier swept them up and waved them under the boy's nose.

"You were heard playing the sacred music. And now I find this! This is a copy of the sacred music itself! It is written in the hand of a boy! Now, where is the original? Where is the music you stole?"

The boy blinked back his tears.

"We didn't steal it!" his father said. "We didn't even see any music!"

"You are not telling the truth!" the soldier thundered. "I am one of the Pope's soldiers. And he has said that anyone who steals this sacred music can be sent to prison!"

"Papa!" the boy cried. "Tell him what happened! Tell him I did not take anything out of the chapel!"

"We are strangers in Rome," the father began. "We come from Austria—"

"I don't care where you come from!" the soldier snapped. "You stole the music!"

"I *heard* the music," the boy said. "And when I came home, I wrote it down."

"Impossible!" the soldier said. "That music is quite old and difficult to listen to. Nobody could remember it well enough to write it all down. You are not telling the truth!"

"I did remember it. I did remember it," the boy sobbed.

"Impossible!" the soldier said. "Now, let's start at the beginning. When you first went into the chapel, what did you do?"

"The music started just as we entered the chapel," the boy said.

"Aha!" the soldier cried. "That proves you are not telling the truth. The first thing everyone does is to look at the ceiling—at Michelangelo's famous paintings, the most famous paintings in all the world. Nobody hears the music at first! Now, tell the truth, boy. Didn't you first see the paintings?"

"What paintings?" the boy asked.

The soldier stared at him. "What paintings!" He shook with anger. "You little thief! You are showing disrespect for—"

The boy's father grabbed the soldier's arm. "Sir, my son Wolfgang just doesn't see."

"What? Is he blind?"

"No, no. I mean, sir, he *can* see. And yet he does not. We ride in the country, and he does not see a single tree. We go through a city, and he does not see the buildings. Everything comes to him through his ears!"

"I cannot believe he did not see the paintings," the soldier said. He stared at the boy. "If what you say is true and you did not see them, you are a very strange child. I don't understand this at all!"

The boy's father shook his head. "He is not strange. He is a genius."

The soldier pursed his lips. "Well, we shall see about this. I will leave a guard at the front door to see that you do not leave this house. I will find someone who knows more about music than I do. He will question the boy."

Later in the day, a message came for Wolfgang and his father. It was from a high church official. The message told them to come to his home that evening and to bring along the music Wolfgang had written down.

When Wolfgang and his father entered the official's home, they found that many people were there. They were led into a large room, glittering with lights. A large pianolike instrument, called a clavichord, stood at one end of the room. Wolfgang's father noticed that many of the people were people he had seen singing in the Sistine Chapel choir when he and his son had heard the music. The crowd was hushed as they entered.

One of the singers stepped forward. "I am Signor Christofori," he said. "I am to judge whether or not you stole the sacred music. Would you please hand over what you have written?"

Wolfgang had been holding the sheets of music rolled up in his hand. He gave them to Signor Christofori.

Signor Christofori unrolled the music. He followed the notes, humming to himself as he read. As he read the music from the sheets, he became more and more excited. At one part he walked rapidly to the clavichord and picked out the notes so that they tinkled loudly throughout the crowded, quiet room. When he had finished, Signor Christofori looked up.

He held up his hand. To the crowd in the room he said, "This music, written in the hand of this young boy, is indeed the sacred music. It is correct, note for note."

Then Signor Christofori looked sadly at young Wolfgang. "I am afraid, young man, that this proves you stole the sacred music. We shall have to report this. You and your father may have to go to prison. I shall recommend mercy because you are so young, but—"

Wolfgang, tears welling up in his eyes again, interrupted, "But sir! I did not steal any music. I heard the sacred music. I loved it. I remembered it when I returned home. The music you just read is what I remembered. Really, it is!"

Wolfgang's father put his arm on his son's shoulder. "The boy tells the truth, sir," he said.

Signor Christofori was impressed. The boy seemed sincere. He turned to talk in low tones to several of the others in the room. For a moment, the room buzzed with talk and excitement. Then Signor Christofori held up his hand again, signaling for quiet.

"Young man," he said. "You seem to speak the truth. It is also true that the original of this music you say you remembered is not missing from the Sistine Chapel. So we cannot say that you stole it. Perhaps you borrowed it and somehow returned it to the chapel. But even that would be against the rules. Even I am not allowed to take the sacred music from the chapel. But you say you remembered it. All right. If you remembered that sacred music, you are a genius. Let us see if you are a genius."

Signor Christofori strode to the clavichord and beckoned the other singers in the room to join him. He turned to Wolfgang and his father.

"We shall play and sing a very difficult piece of music. After we are finished, we shall ask the young lad to play it back for us. If he succeeds, then we shall believe that he did not steal the sacred music. We shall believe that he indeed remembered it." Signor Christofori smiled. He did not believe that Wolfgang would be able to do it.

"Are you willing to take this test?"

Wolfgang's father answered for him. "Yes, he is willing. My boy is a genius, I tell you. Make it as hard as you want. He will play it back for you."

The singers began. It *was* a difficult piece of music. And Wolfgang had never heard it before. He listened intently. The eyes of everyone in the room were on the thirteen-year-old boy as the sounds of the notes and the strange harmonies were heard. The music lasted for half an hour. Then the last note sounded. It was time for the test.

Young Wolfgang went to the clavichord and sat down.

"I cannot sing all the parts at once. Will it be all right if I just hum the main parts while I play?" he asked.

Signor Christofori nodded.

Then Wolfgang began to play. Note for note it was correct. When a main singing part came, his young voice hummed the melody while his nimble fingers tumbled the background notes out of the golden clavichord. The room was silent. Signor Christofori looked at the young boy with astonishment. Finally, Wolfgang came to the end. It had been perfect.

"It's a miracle!" exclaimed Signor Christofori. And after a moment's stunned silence, the people in the room burst into loud applause.

Signor Christofori went to the boy and put his arm on his shoulder. "Your father is right, young man. You *are* a genius."

Wolfgang blushed. He leaned toward Signor Christofori's ear.

"I cheated,"
    he whispered.

The singer stepped back in shocked surprise. His face grew red.

"What? Cheated? Did you already know this piece of music?"

"No, no," Wolfgang said. "I mean I cheated on the sacred music."

Signor Christofori became more angry.

"Oh. So you did steal the sacred music after all?"

"No, sir. But I did not remember it all the first time I heard it. You see, I went back to the chapel on Friday to hear it again so that I could fill in the places I had forgotten. I cheated. I had to hear it two times."

There was a dead silence for a moment. Then Signor Christofori and everyone else in the room roared with laughter. Still laughing, the singer patted Wolfgang's head. "Never mind, young man. It is still a miracle."

So Wolfgang did not go to prison. Instead, the Pope summoned him and awarded him an honor called "The Order of the Golden Spur." He also gave Wolfgang a title: "Signor Cavaliere."

The boy in the story really lived. And the story is true, too. The boy's full name was Wolfgang Amadeus Mozart.

Those who know about music will say that Mozart could hear and remember music in his head better than any person who ever lived. You will hear Mozart's own music many times in your life. And for many people, his music becomes more beautiful each time they hear it.

Mozart did not live long. He died in his home country, Austria, when he was only thirty-five years old, a few years after the United States of America became a nation. But even in his short life, Mozart traveled to many parts of Europe and wrote six hundred and twenty-six pieces of music. He was such an amazing genius that he wrote his first music, and played it on the clavichord, when he was only five years old.

Listen to Mozart's music. You may love it, too.

First page
of a Mozart string quintet
in Mozart's own handwriting

More To Read

Mozart the Wonder Boy by Opal Wheeler and Sybil Deucher. Published by E. P. Dutton & Co., Inc., New York, 1941.

Mozart by Reba Paeff Mirsky. Published by Follett Publishing Company, Chicago, 1960.

Bronze statue of Mozart as a boy by Ernest Barrias

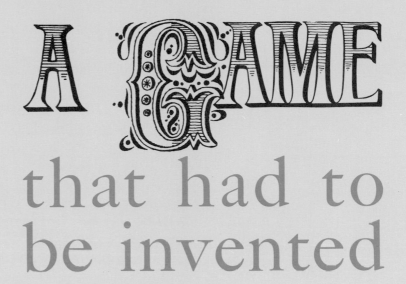

A GAME

that had to be invented

"Men, something must be done immediately," the director of the Springfield YMCA said. "We are losing too many pupils."

All the instructors nodded. The situation was serious. If attendance kept shrinking, some of the instructors might lose their jobs.

"Attendance usually drops off in winter," someone said.

"That's just the point. We have to find something to keep the boys interested when the weather is bad. There must be something they can do indoors that will be fun and exciting," the director replied.

"Something like football or baseball, for instance," one of them pointed out.

"Some kind of team game for indoors looks like our answer," suggested Jim, one of the instructors.

BY KATHERINE B. GORDON

His voice sounded steady enough when he made the suggestion, but he felt nervous inside. Jim was one of the youngest instructors. He would probably be among the first to lose his job if attendance didn't pick up.

"Great idea, Jim, but what game?" someone asked.

"There just isn't a team game that can be played in an area as small as a gymnasium," another said.

"We'll have to invent one!" Jim replied. "I'll see if I can come up with something."

Back in his room after the meeting, Jim realized how hard it would be to invent a new game. He had been quick to suggest a solution all right. But now what was he going to do about it?

Jim spent all his free time during the next week deep in plans, diagrams, and papers. Nothing he came up with seemed right!

He really had a problem!

Football wouldn't work indoors at all. Jim had tried variations on it first. Then he tried baseball. But the gym was too small for that. He had to hurry, or soon there would be no boys left at all.

Finally, Jim had an idea that he thought might work. He went to the YMCA building superintendent for help.

"Can you get me two boxes about this size?" he said, using his hands to show the size he needed.

"What for?" the superintendent asked.

"I'm working on a new game and I need boxes to kick a football into," Jim answered.

The superintendent thought for a moment. Then he said, "I don't have any boxes, but I have a couple of peach baskets down in the storeroom. Would they do?"

"Well, I'll give them a try," Jim answered.

Early the next morning, Jim went to the gymnasium to try out his new idea. The superintendent had left the peach baskets outside. Jim picked them up and walked into the large room. He looked around the gymnasium. He put the baskets down in front of him and tried to decide what would be the best place for them.

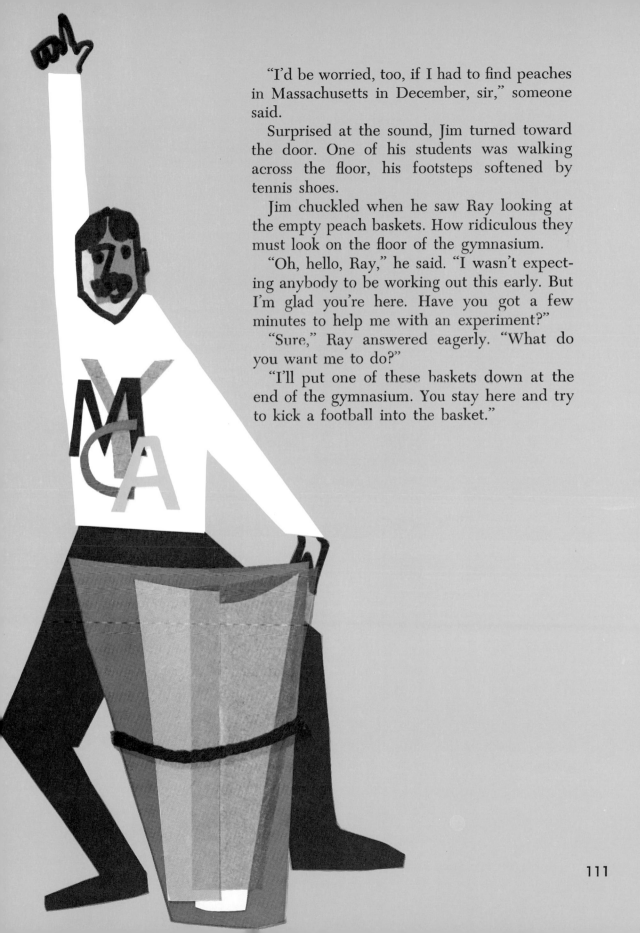

"I'd be worried, too, if I had to find peaches in Massachusetts in December, sir," someone said.

Surprised at the sound, Jim turned toward the door. One of his students was walking across the floor, his footsteps softened by tennis shoes.

Jim chuckled when he saw Ray looking at the empty peach baskets. How ridiculous they must look on the floor of the gymnasium.

"Oh, hello, Ray," he said. "I wasn't expecting anybody to be working out this early. But I'm glad you're here. Have you got a few minutes to help me with an experiment?"

"Sure," Ray answered eagerly. "What do you want me to do?"

"I'll put one of these baskets down at the end of the gymnasium. You stay here and try to kick a football into the basket."

Jim took a football out of one of the lockers and tossed it to Ray. Then he grabbed a peach basket and carried it back to the wall.

Stepping up to the spot his instructor had indicated, Ray eyed the football and then the peach basket. It sure looked a long way from where he was standing.

"I'm ready when you are," Jim called.

Ray's toe connected with the ball. It was a good kick, except for one thing. The ball missed the basket completely!

"Boy, I'm glad the fellows didn't see that!" Ray's face reddened with embarrassment.

Jim didn't hear what Ray said. He was thinking about this new game. Kicking a football into a peach basket was too hard. No one would be able to do it. There must be some other way.

"Maybe I *should* have used boxes," he said out loud.

"Boxes?"

Ray's question snapped Jim's thoughts back to the present.

"I'm sorry, Ray. My mind was somewhere else. I have another idea. Let's try a soccer ball instead. There's one in the locker. See if you can toss it into the basket."

Jim got the soccer ball and threw it to Ray.

Ray took aim and tossed it toward the basket. It landed with a plop right in the center of the basket.

"Good shot," Jim called out.

"Aw, that was easy," Ray said, smiling.

"Almost too easy," Jim replied.

"What's all this about?" Ray asked as Jim came walking toward him.

"I'm trying to work out a new game for you boys," Jim answered. "We need some kind of game to play indoors during bad weather. But it doesn't look as if this one is going to work. It's too hard to get a football into these baskets."

"And it's too easy to get a soccer ball in," Ray admitted.

"You're right," Jim agreed. "I'll have to try something else."

Jim looked at the peach baskets. Then he glanced around the gymnasium.

Suddenly, Jim's eyes lit up. "I've got it!" he shouted. "Come on, Ray, give me a hand with these baskets."

Soon the gymnasium was ready for Jim to explain his new game to the boys and to the other instructors. One basket hung at each end of the gymnasium, about ten feet above the ground. The object of the game was to try to toss the soccer ball into the baskets.

The boys loved the new game. It required teamwork, skill, and accuracy to get the ball into a hanging peach basket. They spent hours at a time in the gymnasium trying to work out new ways to play the game.

There was no longer any attendance problem. Jim had solved the problem by inventing a new game which he called basketball.

Jim, the instructor in this story who invented the game of basketball, was James A. Naismith.

The game of basketball has become so popular that it is not only played in gymnasiums in bad weather, but it is played in all kinds of weather, indoors and out, in playgrounds, alleys, driveways, and empty lots. The ball has changed in size, and new skills for shooting baskets have been developed, but the rules are almost the same as when Jim first invented the game over seventy years ago.

Jim Naismith's proudest moment came in 1936 when he was honored at the Olympic Games in Berlin as the inventor of basketball.

Just a few years ago the United States issued a four-cent postage stamp to honor James A. Naismith and the game of basketball. Have you seen it? Maybe you have one in your stamp collection.

More To Read

Basketball's Greatest Stars by Al Hirshberg. Published by G. P. Putnam's Sons, New York, 1963.

Basketball's Greatest Teams by Al Hirshberg. Published by G. P. Putnam's Sons, New York, 1966.

THE ROAD TO
Waterloo

By Jean Carper

We crouched low behind the ship's railing and held our muskets close to us. Through the gray haze of dawn came the call from a nearby ship, "Identify yourselves."

My heart jumped. Was our plan to fail now? On board our ship was the Emperor of France. I had been a soldier in his army for many years. I had been with him when his dreams for spreading his empire to all Europe had ended in defeat. I had grieved when he was taken from his throne and sent to the Island of Elba as a punishment. Now those of us who were still loyal to him had rescued him from his island prison and were taking him back to France to help him recapture his throne. Everything had gone smoothly until now. But why was this other ship stopping us? Had the Emperor's escape been discovered already?

We gave no answer. We could hear only the sound of hushed voices and shuffling feet on our deck.

"Be ready to fire," whispered our captain.

Again came the voice, "Ahoy! Ahoy there! Who are you? Answer or we'll fire!"

Our captain stepped up behind me and gripped the railing. He whispered nervously to the man who squatted beside me, "What shall I answer, sire? If they guess that you are on board, they will sink us for sure."

"Answer him, but don't let him know I am on board!" The words were stern. I quivered with excitement. The man crouching close to me was the Emperor himself!

Our captain shouted back, "We are the *In-constant*. And who are you?"

"Oh, greetings, my good captain. We are the *Zephyr*. We are patrolling these waters on the lookout for the Emperor. There is a rumor that he may try to escape from the Island of Elba and return to France."

"I have heard no such rumor," replied our captain.

"Why are you sailing so fast toward France?" The tone was suspicious.

My finger tightened on the trigger of my musket.

"We are merely going for supplies as we do every month," our captain answered.

"All right. You are free to go. And happy journey!"

We watched silently as the *Zephyr* faded like a ghost into the morning mist. Then the Emperor and I stood up.

The Emperor barely reached my chin. But he looked strong and he had a powerful voice.

"Were you frightened?" he asked.

"A little, sire."

"No need to be afraid," he said.

I spoke boldly, "We shall soon land in France, and the French people will welcome you back to your throne."

"I hope so," replied the Emperor. "But I have many enemies in France. We will have to fight those who captured me and made me a prisoner on the Island of Elba. King Louis has many friends."

"You have many more, especially the soldiers," I replied.

"We shall soon know." He walked away with his hands clasped behind his back.

No one saw us land on the southern coast of France.

The Emperor sent a detail of soldiers to a nearby fort. "Find out if the commander is friendly. If he is, tell him that we have arrived."

We settled down on the beach. Hours passed and our soldiers did not return. It became dark and we made campfires from driftwood. Suddenly, we heard footsteps slushing through the sand. An old man with a wild look on his face stumbled into our camp.

"Emperor! Emperor!" he cried. "I heard you were here and came to warn you. The commander at the fort is loyal to the King. He has taken your soldiers prisoner and has sent messengers to warn the King that you are back in France."

"Then quick! We must travel with great speed!" ordered the Emperor. "We must start for Paris at once!"

On the first day of our march we passed through several towns. To our surprise, no one shot at us or cheered us. The people just stared curiously.

Then we trudged over snow-laden trails that wound around mountain peaks. My feet were numb. I was afraid I would slip and fall.

At last we reached the outskirts of a town. The Emperor signaled us to halt.

"Do you hear those church bells ringing in the distance?" he asked. "It is a bad sign. Someone has sighted us and now sounds the alarm. Be careful. The townspeople may shoot at us."

Cautiously, we marched into the town. Some people suddenly dashed toward us. I raised my musket. The Emperor drew back to give the signal to fire.

But the people shouted happily, "Long live the Emperor! Welcome back!"

The townspeople fell to their knees before him. They kissed the hem of his long coat. They kissed his sword. An old blind soldier begged to touch him. The Emperor, with a broad smile, patted the soldier on the back.

"But what were the bells we heard?" the Emperor asked.

"Why, only bells tolling for a funeral, sire," answered an old man.

We marched through the town, past the cheering people, and on toward Paris.

Just outside a nearby village we ran into trouble. A soldier from the front of our column ran breathlessly back to the Emperor. "The King's troops block our way."

"I will send an officer to talk with them. They must let us through," said the Emperor.

An officer ran toward the enemy lines. He returned shortly with bad news. "The commander says he is loyal to the King. He says he will take you prisoner or shoot you if you resist."

The Emperor's eyes blazed. "I once commanded those very same troops. We will see if they have nerve enough to shoot me."

Then he did a strange and bold thing. He stepped out from our ranks and walked alone toward the King's soldiers.

The commander saw him and yelled, "There he is! Fire!"

The soldiers seemed paralyzed. Not one pulled a trigger. The Emperor stepped closer. Still no one fired.

The Emperor opened wide his heavy overcoat. He slapped his chest and shouted, "Here I am! If there is any man among you who can kill me, shoot now!"

The soldiers trembled in awful silence. Then one of them ran toward the Emperor, shouting, "Down with the King! Long live the Emperor!"

Hundreds of others followed. With whoops of joy the soldiers ran to the Emperor and formed in ranks behind him.

All along the route to Paris, more soldiers joined us every day.

Citizens lined the streets to cheer us.

At last we were just outside Paris. We halted, waiting for the King's troops to attack us.

We expected the battle to begin any minute.

Then a messenger rode up to the Emperor and handed him a newspaper. Our Emperor read in a loud voice, "King Louis the Eighteenth and the Royal Family fled from Paris last night. They escaped under the cover of darkness when they heard the Emperor and his troops were nearing Paris. His Majesty the Emperor once more sits on the throne of France."

We all cheered loudly and threw our hats in the air.

We entered Paris in great celebration. Cannons roared a salute, and we sang as we marched. Some citizens wept quietly. Others crowded around the Emperor. When we reached the palace, the crowd lifted the Emperor onto their shoulders and carried him to the throne. He was once again the leader of France.

The Emperor of France in this story was Napoleon Bonaparte, a brilliant military leader. At one time his empire covered most of western and central Europe.

This story happened in March, 1815. Although Napoleon regained his throne, he did not keep it for very long. On June 18 of that same year he was defeated by the British at the Battle of Waterloo. This was one of the most important battles in history because it marked the end of Napoleon's power. Today, when someone is defeated or fails to achieve a goal, we say that he has met his Waterloo. Napoleon was captured and sent to the faraway island of St. Helena, where he died six years later.

Napoleon gave many things to the people of France. He made important changes in education and in government. His laws, which were called the Code of Napoleon, still exist in France today.

More To Read

The Emperor and the Drummer Boy by Ruth Robbins. Published by Parnassus Press, Berkeley, Calif., 1962.

Napoleon crossing the Alps, a painting by Jacques-Louis David.

THE DOG THAT

By Jeannette Covert Nolan

Two riders walked their horses slowly across the hilltop and gazed down into the meadow. All morning Florence had been riding through her father's large estate with Mr. Giffard, an old family friend. The brisk exercise had loosened her brown hair from its ribbons. The fresh air had reddened her cheeks.

Florence turned in the saddle and spoke to Mr. Giffard.

"Let's stop here for a minute," she suggested.

Mr. Giffard drew up beside her. "Are you tired? Has the ride been too long for you?"

"Oh, no," Florence smiled. "But from the hill, we can watch old Roger's collie dog, Cap, herding the sheep. He's a wonderful dog and I love to watch him at work."

"Roger is lucky to have a dog like Cap," Mr. Giffard agreed.

WAS TO BE KILLED

Florence looked down into the meadow. But something was wrong! Cap was nowhere in sight. The sheep were wandering off in all directions. Old Roger was racing around waving his arms like a windmill at the straying sheep.

"Come, Mr. Giffard," Florence said. "Something must be wrong with Cap! Let's find out what has happened."

Florence and Mr. Giffard galloped down to the meadow.

"Are you having trouble, Roger?" Mr. Giffard asked the old farmer.

"Ah, sir, I am," Roger replied. "These pesky sheep won't mind me at all."

"But where is Cap?" asked Florence.

"In my house, missy. He's tied up and locked in. Poor Cap!

His leg is badly hurt. I'm afraid I shall have to do away with him to end his misery."

"Oh, Roger, you don't mean you're going to *kill* Cap!" Florence cried.

"I don't know what else to do, Miss Florence," Roger said. "Cap is in terrible pain. His sheepherding days are over. He'll never be able to run again. But now please excuse me. I must chase my sheep. They've wandered away again!"

As old Roger hurried to follow his sheep, Florence turned to Mr. Giffard. "I'm going to Roger's house," she said. "I know where the key is. Surely I can do *something* for Cap. At least, I can try."

"I'll go with you," Mr. Giffard offered.

The injured dog lay stretched on the floor of Roger's little kitchen. At the sound of the key in the lock, he barked fiercely. But when he saw Florence and heard her murmur, "Dear Cap! Quiet, Cap!" he feebly wagged his tail.

Mr. Giffard bent over Cap and gently examined the leg which was bleeding and swollen.

"Is it really broken?" Florence asked anxiously.

"I can't tell yet. Stand back," Mr. Giffard warned. "He might bite you."

Mr. Giffard went on examining the dog's leg. "The bone is not broken," he said. "But the muscles have been strained and torn, and the flesh has been cut. Hot cloths should be applied."

"I'll boil some water," Florence said. "The kettle's on the stove."

She jumped to her feet and took Roger's cotton shirt from a peg on the wall. She ripped the shirt into squares of cloth and folded the squares to make soft pads. Then she heated the water on the stove.

For more than an hour, Florence and Mr. Giffard applied the hot pads to Cap's leg. The wounded dog lay very still.

"That should do for today," Mr. Giffard said. "I'll bandage him up. But he ought to have another treatment tomorrow."

"I'll come tomorrow, and every day until Cap is better!" Florence promised.

"You are a good nurse, Florence," Mr. Giffard said.

"That's what I want to be!" she exclaimed. "I want to study nursing and work in a hospital, caring for sick people, making them comfortable, and helping them to get well. That's my main ambition."

Mr. Giffard seemed surprised. "A fine ambition, indeed! Have you talked with your parents about it?"

"Yes, often," she answered. "They say it's nonsense and that I must forget it. Papa says that hospitals are dismal, dirty places, and that nursing is work for men, not for women."

"True enough," said Mr. Giffard. "Our hospitals are in a dreadful state and the nurses are mostly rough, uneducated men who have never been trained for their tasks. Your father is a gentleman, Florence. And the daughters of English gentlemen do not become hospital nurses."

"I want to be a nurse, even though papa is against it. It's what I want more than anything else," Florence replied.

When Florence reached home, she told her father about Cap.

He listened gravely. "Those torn muscles may mend in a month or two," he said. "But Cap will probably always be lame. A lame dog is not of much use to a sheepherder. I'm afraid we'll have to get rid of Cap."

"Cap won't be lame!" Florence declared. "I'll cure him, papa. In a week I'll have him running around as good as new."

"I doubt that you, or anyone else, could perform a cure like that in a week's time, Florence."

"I will!" she said. "Just wait and see!"

It seemed to Florence that the next week streaked by like lightning. She had made a promise to her father, and to herself. Here was her chance to prove that she had a real talent for nursing!

Every day, Florence went to visit Cap. She put hot pads and fresh bandages on his leg. She helped him to get up from the floor, and then to walk slowly around Roger's kitchen. Each day Cap was a little better, but he limped as if his leg was still sore. He seemed afraid to run.

He had to run! It was his only chance.

On the sixth morning old Roger watched as Florence applied the hot pads. He was not very hopeful about Cap's recovery.

"He will never herd sheep again, missy," Roger said sadly.

"We must have faith, Roger," Florence said. "Tomorrow is the end of the week, and papa is coming here with me. I want you to leave your kitchen door open. I have a plan, and I don't believe that Cap will disappoint me."

Florence didn't show how nervous she was. Cap had to run by tomorrow, and he was still limping. If only her plan would work!

The next day, Florence and her father rode their horses toward Roger's house. Florence was frightened. Suppose her plan should fail? Suppose Cap should disappoint her? She felt that somehow her whole future was at stake. And if Cap wouldn't run, what would her father do with him?

As they neared the house, Florence saw Cap peering out through the open doorway. Roger was standing behind him. Well, this is the test, Florence thought.

"Stop here, papa," she said. Then in a loud clear voice, she called, "Here, Cap! Come here!"

Cap stood in the doorway. At first he did not move. He began to wag his tail and then slowly he stepped out into the yard.

Trying to hide her disappointment, Florence called to him again. "Run, Cap. Run! I know you can do it. Please! Run to me!"

There was a moment's silence. Then Cap barked joyfully and bounded across the lawn to meet her—running fast on all fours without the slightest trace of a limp.

Florence leaped from her saddle and threw her arms around Cap.

"Why, sir, he's fit as a fiddle!" Roger cried, with a look of surprise on his face. "It's a miracle, sir, and it's all Miss Florence's doing."

"It's not a miracle, Roger," Florence said. "I just took care of Cap the way any nurse would—and I prayed a lot." Then she turned to her father. "Papa, won't you let me buy some books about nursing and medicine, now?" she pleaded.

"Nursing and medicine!" her father sighed. "That's all you ever think of! But very well. You've done a good job with Cap. Buy the books and consider them a reward from Cap."

Florence, the young girl in this story, was Florence Nightingale, whose dream of becoming a nurse came true.

At about the same time that the Civil War was being fought in the United States, another war was being fought between Great Britain and Russia. It was called the Crimean War. Florence Nightingale gathered a small group of nurses together and went to take care of the British soldiers who were wounded in the Crimean War. Each night Florence walked through the dark halls of the British hospital, caring for the sick and wounded. As she walked, she carried a lamp to see her way. The wounded soldiers called her their "Lady with the Lamp."

When she returned to England, Florence started a home for nurses in London. She soon became famous all over the world because of her methods of caring for the sick and needy.

Florence Nightingale changed the nursing profession to the respected group it is today.

More To Read

Florence Nightingale by Ruth Fox Hume. Published by Random House, New York, 1960.

Great Women of Medicine by Ruth Fox Hume. Published by Random House, New York, 1964.

Miss Florence Nightingale
at Embley
December 28th 1857.

Little Sure

By Katherine Gehm

"Do you mean to tell me this is the first time you have ever been in a shooting gallery?" the manager shouted.

Annie had never seen anyone so surprised. She looked directly up at the man in charge of the gallery. "Yes, sir," she replied softly. "This is the first time I've ever been in Cincinnati, too. I'm visiting my sister. I didn't know that people shot rifles just for fun until today."

The manager paced the floor excitedly. "Do you realize what you have done?" he thundered.

"Did I do something wrong?" Annie asked meekly.

"Wrong? Wrong?" he bellowed. Then turning abruptly to the other shooters, he moaned, "She's just hit the bull's-eye six times in a row and asks if she's done something wrong!" He slapped his forehead twice with the palm of his hand.

"Isn't that what you told me to do?" Annie asked and nervously turned to look for her sister.

Her sister hurried over, grabbed Annie, and hugged her tight.

"What did I do wrong?" Annie

asked again.

"You didn't do anything wrong, miss! It's just that not very many people can shoot that well. You're a great shot!"

People began crowding around Annie in wonder.

"Where did you learn to shoot like that?" the excited manager asked.

"By shooting birds at home," Annie explained, still confused by all

 Shot

the attention she was getting. "I had to hunt for food for my family."

"You're one of the best shots I've seen in all the years that I have had this gallery. And you're only a kid, too!" The manager almost danced with excitement.

"Just beginner's luck, maybe," someone shouted. "Let her try to hit the ducks!"

Annie turned to the targets. She saw a row of metal ducks. She wondered why anyone thought it would be hard to hit them.

"Yeah!" a woman called out. "Let's see her try to hit the ducks!"

The manager handed her another gun. "Try to hit them!" he said while he pulled a lever to start the ducks moving from side to side.

Confidently, Annie balanced the rifle in her hands, swung it to her shoulder, sighted along the barrel, and fired six shots quickly. One-two-three-four-five-six ducks fell one after another!

For a second nobody said anything. Then, suddenly, everyone began to cheer.

"What about having a shooting match between Annie and Frank Butler?" someone asked.

Annie didn't know who Frank Butler was, but her sister told her that he was the best shot in Cincinnati. "He makes his living entertaining people with his shooting," she told Annie.

"Wouldn't it be fun to make a living by shooting for people's entertainment?" said Annie, aloud.

Happily, Annie accepted the suggestion to have a match with Butler.

The following day when the manager of the shooting gallery came to tell her the match was scheduled for Friday night, Annie's eyes glistened. It was still a mystery to her, though, why everyone was so excited. Shooting metal ducks was easy!

On Friday evening her sister brought Annie to the place where the match was to be held. There was a

crowd waiting when they arrived. News of the match had spread all over town. Annie looked around. There seemed to be hundreds of people milling about.

One lone man was standing nearby. He looked older than Annie, maybe eight or ten years, and he had on a fancy jacket that made her feel ashamed of her homemade dress.

The manager of the shooting gallery greeted her pleasantly, then turned to the man with the fancy jacket. "Mr. Butler, here is the young lady who challenges you."

Frank Butler looked at Annie's face and at the two braids of chestnut hair falling on her shoulders.

Then he turned to the manager. "What's the matter with you, Jake? Professionals don't take advantage of youngsters!"

"You haven't seen her shoot, Frank. She's good."

"But she's only a kid!"

"She's older than she looks, Frank."

"I'm sorry, Jake, I won't do it!"

Annie felt her face turning red. Her knees began to wobble.

He thinks I'm just a child, she thought.

She wished she had never left her home to come to Cincinnati. At home she could take her rifle and tramp by herself through the woods and the cornfields hunting quail, grouse, and pigeons. That was what she liked to do best.

Frank Butler didn't think she could shoot! That was it! He didn't think she knew how! Well, she would show him!

Looking straight at him, she asked, "Are you afraid, Mr. Butler?"

Frank Butler's face flushed. "It just isn't fair to you, Annie," he said.

"I'm willing," she answered.

Butler shrugged his shoulders. "All right, but don't expect me to make it easy for you."

He then turned to the manager. "Okay, Jake, let's start."

The manager explained to Annie how the match would work. "You will shoot at clay targets that move through the air," he said. "You will take turns, each shooting at one target at a time. Whoever's turn it is to shoot will get ready, and call out 'Pull!' A target will be thrown into the air, and you will fire at it."

Annie nodded.

The manager went on, "If you hit the target, the referee will shout, 'Dead!' If you miss, the referee will shout, 'Miss!' Whoever has hit the most targets after twenty-five shots will be the winner. Do you understand, Annie?"

"Yes, sir."

They took their places at the line. Frank Butler was to shoot first.

"Pull!" he called and a target sailed into the air.

He swung the gun to his shoulder and fired.

"Dead!" called the referee, as the target fell.

Now it was Annie's turn. She could not keep her hands from shaking and did not see how she could hold the gun steady. The stillness of the people all around her made her feel embarrassed. She knew that everyone was looking at her.

She wanted to go back home, but she knew she couldn't do that. In one fleeting second she put everything else out of her mind and imagined she was in the woods back home shooting at quail.

"Pull!" she called.

A target flew up.

Annie fired quickly.

"Dead!" called the referee.

Round after round Frank Butler and Annie kept taking turns and never missing. As the match went on, the look on Frank Butler's face changed from amusement to surprise to respect for Annie's shooting.

Finally, it was the last round.

Butler stepped up to the line. "Pull," he said.

The target flew through the air. Frank Butler fired.

The target swept past.

"Miss!" shouted the referee.

The crowd buzzed excitedly.

Now it was Annie's final shot. The crowd became silent again.

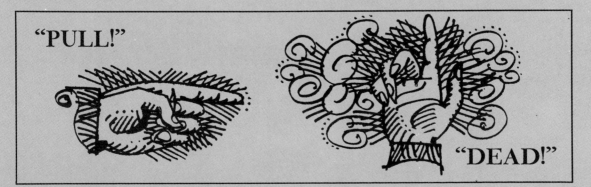

"PULL!" "DEAD!"

"PULL!" she called and pressed the trigger.

"DEAD!" called the referee.

Annie had won the match! She had beaten Frank Butler! The crowd gathered around her, cheering and shouting her name.

Annie looked at Frank Butler who was standing alone. She wondered if he was angry with her. What right did she have to beat the best shot in Cincinnati?

She started to walk toward Butler.

He came over to meet her. "Annie, that was fine shooting."

"Thank you, Mr. Butler."

Frank Butler looked at Annie for a moment. Then a wide grin spread across his face. "You know, you're a good enough shot to go on the stage," he said.

"Oh, Mr. Butler, that would be wonderful!" she replied.

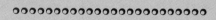 

Annie in this story was Phoebe Anne Oakley Mozee, who later became known as Annie Oakley.

Annie and Frank Butler were soon married. And they became partners on the stage, too. Together they traveled to many parts of the world and amazed people with their shooting.

Annie was such a remarkable shooter that she could shoot things sticking out of people's mouths without hurting them, or hit a playing card from a long way off with only the thin edge of the card facing her.

Because of her size and her shooting, Annie was nicknamed, "Little Sure Shot."

More To Read

Buffalo Bill by Ingri M. and Edgar P. d'Aulaire. Published by
Doubleday & Company, Inc., New York, 1952.

THE
MONSTER'S RIDDLE

BY S. L. BINSTOCK

One day Oedipus, a young man who lived in the city of Corinth, came to ask the oracle a question. The oracle was supposed to know the answers to everything. Oedipus wished to know what life had in store for him.

The oracle said to Oedipus, "Apollo, God of the Sun, commands that you go to the city of Thebes, for there you will find fame and fortune."

Oedipus lost no time preparing for his journey. Thebes was a long distance from Corinth, but Oedipus did not care. His heart was filled with gladness. The god, Apollo, had said that fame and fortune would be his.

He had to travel by foot. This did not cause him any worry, for he was young and strong. As he walked along the hot, dusty road, every tree seemed to wave a leafy greeting, and every bird seemed to sing of the glory which would be his in Thebes. At night he camped under the stars and lay awake for hours, staring up at the heavens and wondering what Apollo had planned for him.

On the third day of his travels when the sun was almost directly overhead in the sky, Oedipus knew that his journey was nearing an end.

I have heard that Thebes is a three-day journey from Corinth, he thought. It cannot be far. I hope that I meet another traveler so I may ask him the distance to Thebes.

Oedipus did not have long to wait for his wish to come true. The road wound up a hill, and when Oedipus reached the top of the hill, he saw not one, but several travelers—men, women, and children, and horses carrying great loads.

They do not seem to be merchants, thought Oedipus. I wonder where so many people are going.

As he approached the travelers, Oedipus could see that they were led by an old man with gray hair and a long gray beard.

"Good day to you, sir," said Oedipus. "May I ask a question of you?"

The old man raised his hand high and the procession halted.

"What is it, my son?" the old man replied.

"I am Oedipus of Corinth. I am on my way to Thebes. I would like to know how far that city is from where we now stand."

Oedipus noticed that the old man stared at him with a look of great surprise on his face. He also noticed that the other travelers, who had been near enough to hear his words, looked at him as if he were some strange creature.

"What have I said to offend you?" asked Oedipus.

The old man smiled and put his hand on Oedipus' shoulder.

"Your words do not offend us, young Oedipus, but they do surprise us. However, I think that you do not know."

"Do not know? Do not know what?" asked Oedipus.

"You do not know that you cannot enter Thebes. No one can. To try may cost you your life."

Oedipus clutched the old man's arm. "Is there some sickness in the city?" he asked.

The old man turned and pointed with his wrinkled arm. "Do you see that mountain in the distance? That is Mount Phicium. To get to Thebes one must pass over that mountain. Once Mount Phicium was a beautiful sight to the people of Thebes and to those traveling there. But now it is a dreaded sight. A monster, known as the Sphinx, now lives on the top of the mountain. The Sphinx has brought great misery to Thebes because no person has been able to enter the city since first she came."

"Then I shall fight this monster," cried Oedipus.

"You have great courage," said the old man. "But you cannot defeat her in combat. Although she has the head of a woman, she has the body of a lion, the wings of an eagle, and the tail of a serpent. There is but one way a person can pass by her and enter the city."

"How is that?" asked Oedipus.

"When she first came upon us, the monster told the people of Thebes that she would not harm anyone *leaving* the city. But she would stop those wishing to enter Thebes and ask them a riddle. If they could answer the riddle, they would pass unharmed. But if they could not supply the answer, she would kill them on the spot."

"Tell me," said Oedipus. "What is this riddle?"

"No one knows what it is," answered the old man. "All those who have heard it have perished. Alas, although many have tried to give the monster the answer to her riddle, none has succeeded. Their bones are scattered about the gates of the city. Thebes is a dying city. Food is scarce. We could not go outside the city to plant in the fields or to hunt for food, for fear that we could not get back inside the gates. No merchant can enter the city to sell us his wares. That is why we are leaving."

Suddenly, Oedipus stepped back a few paces so that he might be able to see the entire group of travelers.

"Friends!" he shouted. "Come back with me to Thebes, for tonight you will sleep in your beloved city. I, Oedipus of Corinth, have been

commanded by the oracle to go to Thebes. The oracle told me that Apollo said I would find fame and fortune there. Surely, the god would not send me to Thebes if he did not have some plan. I know that he means for me to vanquish the Sphinx."

When he had said this, there was much talk among the travelers, but Oedipus could not hear their words.

The old man stepped forward. "We cannot go back with you. This is a difficult journey. If you are killed by the Sphinx, we would have to start again from the beginning. But since you are sent by Apollo, we will not go on with our journey until we learn of your fate. We will camp here, and I will send two young men with you. They can return and tell us if you have succeeded in your mission."

"So be it," replied Oedipus. "I wish to go immediately."

The old man turned to his companions and called two names. Two youths approached the spot where he and Oedipus stood. After the old man explained what was expected of them, the two youths joined Oedipus and the three young men started for Thebes.

When they had nearly reached the top of Mount Phicium, one of the young men turned to Oedipus. "We will go no farther," he said. "You will see the Sphinx when you take a few more steps. If you do defeat her as you think you will, it will be easy for you to run back and tell us. If you are determined to do this, then may the gods be with you." They shook hands, and Oedipus walked on.

Just as his companion had said, Oedipus had taken only a few steps when he reached the top of the mountain and came upon the Sphinx. She was, as the old man had told him, a horrible monster. Even the great courage of Oedipus faltered when he saw her. But remembering the words of the oracle, he walked straight toward her.

The Sphinx had been lying down, but when she saw Oedipus approaching, she raised her lion's body and her serpent's tail began twisting in the air.

"Good day to you young man," the Sphinx said in a cackling voice. "Where are you going?"

"I am going down there," answered Oedipus pointing at the city of Thebes which lay before him at the bottom of the mountain.

"Maybe you will," said the Sphinx. "And maybe you will meet your death if you do not turn around and go back."

"I shall not go back," replied Oedipus. "And I shall not die this day."

"Very well," cackled the monster. "Then I shall ask you my riddle. If you give me the correct answer to the riddle, you may pass on to Thebes. But if you fail to answer it correctly, I shall pounce on you and kill you in an instant."

"Ask your riddle, monster," said Oedipus.

"Here is the riddle," said the Sphinx.

"What has only one voice, but sometimes has four legs, sometimes two legs, and sometimes three legs, and is weakest when it has the most?"

It was a difficult riddle. Oedipus began to think very hard. As he thought, he gazed down at the city and saw that there were many people in the streets of Thebes pointing up to where he and the Sphinx stood. While he watched, more and more people came out of their homes to stare up at them.

Presently the Sphinx said, "I have given you enough time for thought. Do you have the answer to my riddle?"

Suddenly, the answer came into Oedipus' mind as if by magic.

"Yes," cried Oedipus. "I do have your answer. The answer to your riddle is 'MAN.'"

"You have not answered it all," replied the monster. "You must tell me the reasons for your answer."

"A man speaks with one voice," said Oedipus. "When he is an infant, he crawls on his hands and knees. This makes four legs. When he is a young man, he walks on two legs. When he is old, he walks with a cane. This makes three legs. He is weakest when he has the most, because he is weakest when he is an infant and crawls on four legs."

The Sphinx did not expect to hear anyone give the answer to her riddle. When she heard it, she became furious. She flapped

her wings rapidly, and her tail began to twist again. She rolled on the ground in anger until she rolled off the edge of the mountain. She was so angry that she did not think to use her wings. Thus, the Sphinx fell to her death.

The people who had been watching gave forth a cheer that shook the earth.

Oedipus ran to the spot where the two young men waited for him. He told them to return to their friends to say that they could indeed sleep in their city that night.

He then climbed down the mountain. The people of Thebes were already gathered to greet him and carry him into the city. They were so thankful to Oedipus that they made him the King of Thebes. The prophecy of the oracle had come true.

The tales of Oedipus and his many adventures come to us from the legends of ancient Greece. This story is only one of his adventures. These tales have been passed down from father to son for many centuries. Many famous writers have written about Oedipus.

No one knows whether Oedipus really lived or not. But the wonderful stories about him probably will live forever.

More To Read

Adventures of the Greek Heroes by Mollie McLean and Anne Wiseman. Published by Houghton Mifflin Co., Boston, 1961.

Black Mike to the

Rescue

Jimmy sat alone almost hidden by the tall prairie grass. He had tried to be brave in front of Ma and Little Sister, but he was scared. And now that he was alone, he began to cry.

Jimmy and his family had been left behind by the wagon train when one of their horses had run off. By the time they had caught the horse, the other wagons were out of sight. They had followed the tracks to a river. But now their wagon was stuck in the sand of the riverbed. Pa had gone off yesterday to catch up with the wagon train and bring back help.

Pa had promised to be back before sundown yesterday. But he was almost a whole day late already. The family was nearly out of food, and Jimmy had set out to find a rabbit for supper. So far, he hadn't seen any kind of game at all.

What could have happened to Pa? Jimmy wondered. Maybe the Indians have ambushed and killed him! How could they get their wagon out of the sand? And what were they going to do about food?

If only we hadn't come out West, he said to himself. Then he remembered how excited he had been when his folks had decided to sell their farm and move to Oregon, after hearing a man make a speech about it.

Suddenly, Jimmy heard footsteps. He whirled around! Coming

By Enid Johnson

toward him was a strange-looking man with a black beard, wearing a buckskin suit with long fringes down the seams of his trousers. Strapped to his back was a pack made of buffalo skin that bulged with all sorts of things.

"Howdy, stranger," the man said in a kind voice. "Seems like you're in some kind of trouble."

"Y—Y—Yes, Sir," Jimmy replied, wiping his eyes.

"Tell me all about it, son," the man urged.

He seemed so friendly that Jimmy poured out the whole story.

When the stranger heard that Jimmy and his family had nothing to eat but potatoes, he said, "Let's go to your wagon. I've got some meat in my pack that I'll share with you folks, and when your Pa gets back, we'll see what we can do about getting your wagon out of the sand."

"Do you live around here, Mister?" Jimmy asked.

"Not anymore. I used to trap beaver hereabouts and sell their pelts to the fur companies. But the streams are pretty well cleaned out, so I'm going farther west to the mountains, where there's lots of beaver. Now let's go and cook the meat. By the time we've used it all up, I'll surely get a buffer."

Seeing Jimmy's puzzled look, he said, "So you don't know what a 'buffer' is. Well, that's what we trappers call buffalo."

"Are you a mountain man?" Jimmy asked.

"I sure am!" the stranger replied. "They call me 'Black Mike,' because of my black beard."

"My name's Jimmy," the boy said.

"Well, Jimmy, let's go back to that wagon of yours now and have some dinner."

When they reached the wagon, Jimmy noticed that Ma looked at the stranger as though she was scared of him. He *was* kind of rough looking, but Jimmy hoped that Ma would notice his kind blue eyes.

"Ma, this is Mr. Black Mike. Black Mike, this is my Ma."

"Pleased to meet you, Ma'am," Black Mike said. "I was just telling Jimmy that I've got some meat I'd like to share with you folks."

"Thank you, Black Mike. That's very kind of you," Ma said, holding out her hand.

Jimmy saw Black Mike wipe his palm on his jacket before tak-

ing Ma's hand. Black Mike seemed pleased that she wanted to shake hands with him.

Maybe he doesn't often get to talk to a lady like Ma, Jimmy thought.

Jimmy and Black Mike gathered firewood while Ma got the potatoes and coffee ready. When the fire was blazing, Black Mike took long, sharp, pointed sticks from his pack and put the meat on them. Little Sister came out of the door of the wagon when she smelled the meat cooking.

They sat around the fire to eat, and soon they had eaten every scrap.

After dinner, Black Mike stood looking at some things that other travelers had thrown away along the riverbank. "Golly, those people make themselves lots of trouble, with their heavy loads! They bring so much useless stuff along."

"We brought too much, ourselves, but we didn't know any better," Jimmy said. "The man who made a speech about how folks ought to go and settle in Oregon didn't say anything about that. He said lots of things that aren't true, though. Didn't he, Ma? And we believed him."

"He certainly painted a rosy picture of Oregon," Ma agreed.

"Oh, Oregon's a fine place," Black Mike told them. "It's getting there that's bad. What did the fellow say that isn't so, son?"

"Well, for one thing, he said we'd find lots of game along the way. He told us that the plains were 'black with buffalo'—those were his very words. And we haven't seen a buffalo yet! We were figuring on having lots of buffalo meat to eat."

"Just wait," Black Mike said. "You'll be seeing plenty from now on."

Next morning, Jimmy and Black Mike, carrying empty pails, went to get fresh water from a stream that emptied into the river.

"Let's take our rifles along, Jimmy," Black Mike said.

They hadn't gone three miles, when they heard a strange sound, like the bellowing of a big bull.

"Listen, son! Sounds like buffer!"

Soon they saw a procession of huge buffaloes, walking one behind the other, across a grassy hilltop.

"Let's get behind that big rock, Jimmy," Black Mike said. "When we get a chance we'll take a shot at one of them."

Soon they heard the thud-thud of the approaching buffaloes. A moment later, an enormous black head appeared above the long weeds and grass. Jimmy could just make out the animal's horns in its tangled mane. Half-sliding, half-plunging, the great buffalo went into the river. Then it stepped out onto a sand bar, and bent its massive head down to drink. When it raised its head, the boy saw drops of water falling from its wet beard.

Black Mike cocked his rifle. Jimmy cocked his, too. Then the man rested his elbow on his knee, to make his aim steadier. The boy imitated him. Then, putting the stock of his gun against his shoulder, Black Mike sighted the buffalo along the barrel. Jimmy did the same.

Why doesn't he fire? Jimmy wondered. But Black Mike seemed in no hurry.

The buffalo, having drunk all it wanted, began to march slowly over the sands to the other side of the river.

"See that small bare spot just behind his

shoulder?" Black Mike whispered. "That's the place to aim for. Go ahead, son. He's all yours."

Jimmy pressed the trigger.

"Good boy!" Black Mike shouted. "You hit him!"

"Honest?" Jimmy asked. "He doesn't look hit, or even hurt!"

"Look at the bare spot now. See the red dot in the middle of it?"

Jimmy saw that the red dot was growing larger, but still nothing happened.

"Why doesn't he fall?" he asked.

"Wait a bit. He will."

Slowly the huge beast began to totter. Its knees bent under it. Its great head sank to the ground. Then its whole body swayed to one side, and it rolled over on the sand.

"Hurray!" cried Jimmy. "I got a buffalo! Let's go skin him!"

"Hold on, sonny," the trapper warned. "The rest of the herd are coming along. We'd be in a peck of trouble if we got mixed up with them."

A few seconds later, the whole herd came near the place where the dead buffalo lay. Paying no attention to it, each began to drink deeply from the stream.

After what seemed like hours to the boy, the herd of buffaloes turned around and galloped away. They had walked in one straight line, like marching soldiers, when they came to the stream to drink. Now they rushed pell-mell back across the prairie. Their pounding hoofs sounded like thunder.

As soon as the herd had gone, Jimmy and Black Mike began skinning the dead buffalo.

"Your folks are going to be mighty proud of you, son," Black Mike said. "You're a regular Daniel Boone. Now let's fetch some water and get back to the wagon."

They filled their pails and started for the wagon. But they were slowed down by their heavy loads of water and buffalo meat, and it took them some time.

Little Sister ran out to meet them. "Jimmy, Pa's back," she cried happily.

"Did he bring anyone back with him?" Jimmy asked.

"No, he couldn't find the wagon train. There were too many tracks going every which way," she answered. "But he's back and he's safe."

Soon they reached the wagon. Pa smiled at Jimmy and shook hands with Black Mike after Jimmy had introduced them.

"Ma and Little Sister told me about your sharing your meat with them last night," he said. "I'm mighty obliged to you, Black Mike."

"Well, now you'll have enough meat to last quite awhile," Black Mike said. "Jimmy here shot himself a big buffer. And he hit it right in the one spot that kills buffer sure."

Pa thumped Jimmy on the back. "Good boy," he said. "We've got a real hunter in the family. I'm proud of you, son."

Ma was too overcome to speak. But Little Sister jumped up and down and shouted, "Isn't my big brother wonderful?"

"He certainly is," Pa agreed. "At last we'll have some food to tide us over. But I guess we'll have to wait until another wagon train happens along and we can get our wagon out of the sand."

"That might take quite a spell," said Black Mike. "I'll show you how to get that wagon out. You'll be back on the trail in no time."

Young Jimmy, Ma, Pa, and Little Sister were members of a pioneer family going west along the Oregon Trail.

The pioneers would meet in Independence, Missouri. They would form wagon trains and follow the trail across prairies, plains, and mountains, almost all the way to the Pacific Ocean. A trip would take about six months. The pioneers faced many dangers along the trail. They often ran out of food, or were separated from their wagon trains. They faced terrible storms and Indian attacks. Some of the pioneers died along the trail. Others turned back.

Mountain men like Black Mike often came to their rescue, sometimes guiding the pioneers all the way to Oregon.

If you travel today along the land that was once the Oregon Trail, you can still see deep ruts made by wagon wheels.

More To Read

Trails West and Men Who Made Them by Edith Dorian and W. N. Wilson. Published by McGraw-Hill Book Company, New York, 1955.

The First Book of the Oregon Trail by Walter Havighurst. Published by Franklin Watts, Inc., New York, 1960.

Chimney Rock, Nebraska, a landmark of the old Oregon Trail as it looks today.

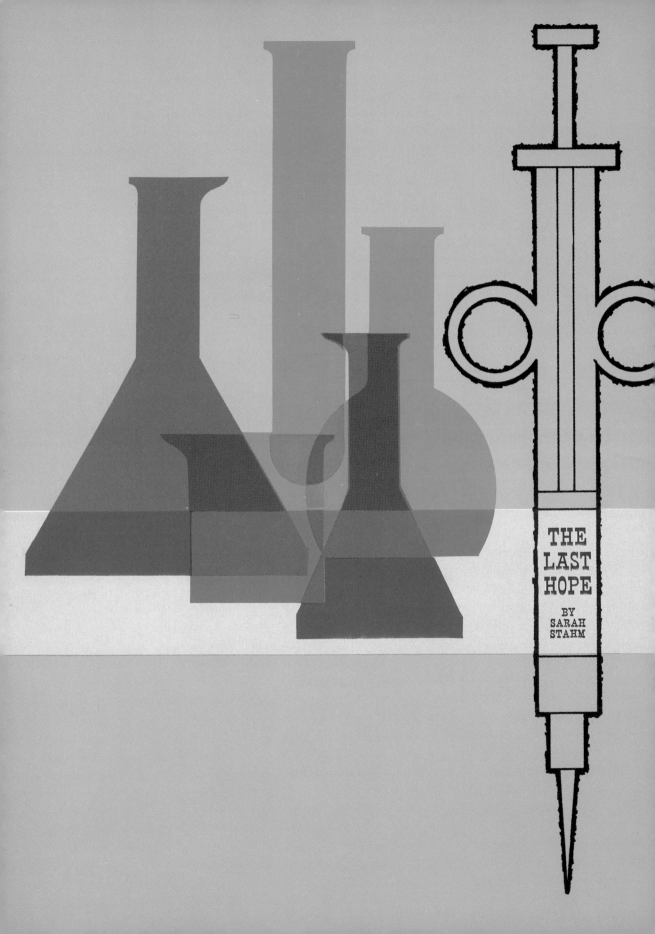

THE
LAST
HOPE

BY
SARAH
STAHM

The doctor sat in his big rocking chair. He had finished his dinner and was resting after a long, hard day. Suddenly, he heard loud banging on the door.

"Doctor, Doctor Weber, let me in! Open the door, please hurry!"

The doctor jumped up from his comfortable chair and rushed to the door. One of his patients was standing on the porch. Her face was flushed. Her eyes were red and swollen. She was breathless from running, but managed to gasp, "My son, Joseph, has been bitten by a dog. Come quickly!"

"Now, Mrs. Meister, control yourself. A little nip will heal quickly," the doctor consoled her. "Come in and rest for a minute. Then you can tell me the whole story."

"But you don't understand, Doctor. The dog had foam all around its mouth and chin. Its eyes were wild and red. I am sure it had rabies."

Doctor Weber argued no longer. These were the signs he dreaded. If Mrs. Meister was right, there was cause for great alarm. He grabbed his bag from the table.

"Come, Mrs. Meister. We will go to see Joseph at once. Get into the wagon while I hitch up the horse."

It was a long ride through the village. To the mother, the ride seemed endless. To the doctor, it seemed hopeless. If the dog had rabies, there was nothing he could do for the child. No cure was known. Nothing helped. Both the person who had been bitten and the dog always died. His only hope was that Mrs. Meister was mistaken—that the dog did not have rabies.

At last, they reached the Meister home. The doctor hurried in to see if he could do anything for Joseph. Mr. Meister sat at the child's bedside. Joseph was lying on the bed, restlessly turning from side to side. He had bites on his face, his arms, and his legs. Doctor Weber counted fourteen bites in all. Gently, he washed the child's wounds and tried to make him comfortable. Joseph began to cry.

"Now, now, you are a big boy," he said to Joseph. "You must be brave. Close your eyes. Try to think of the nicest thing you can. You must be very quiet."

Doctor Weber covered the child and motioned to the parents to follow him into the other room. Joseph's father told him that the dog had been examined.

The examination showed that the dog had rabies.

"My dear Mr. and Mrs. Meister, Joseph is very ill," Doctor Weber said slowly. "He has been bitten in such a way that he cannot be cured. The dog's teeth bit through Joseph's skin. The poison has entered his body. We know of no one who has ever recovered from such an illness."

"No, oh, no!" cried Mrs. Meister. "You cannot let him die. Surely there is something or someone who can help him!"

"If only there were," the doctor said. "But there is nothing anyone can do. No one who can—" His voice trailed off to a whisper. He remembered a report he had read in a science journal a few days before. Someone had claimed to have found a way to prevent rabies in animals. Who was it?

Suddenly, he remembered. Of course, it was Pasteur! Louis Pasteur had announced a vaccine for rabies that worked perfectly on animals. But he had never tried it on humans. Would it work?

"What is it, Doctor? What are you thinking of?" Joseph's father asked excitedly.

"There may be a way to save your son," Doctor Weber answered. "Don't get your hopes up. I cannot be sure. But a scientist in Paris claims to have found a vaccine to prevent rabies in animals. Would you be willing to take Joseph to Paris to talk to Mr. Pasteur?"

"Yes, of course, anything, any place," the father answered quickly.

The next morning, Doctor Weber and the Meisters arrived at Louis Pasteur's laboratory. Joseph was in such pain that he could hardly walk. Pasteur made the child comfortable. Then Pasteur listened while the doctor told him what had happened.

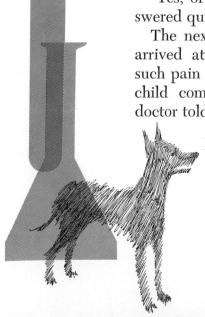

Louis Pasteur looked at Joseph for a long time and then turned to the boy's parents.

"Listen carefully," he said to them. "You must understand what I am about to tell you. For years I have worked on a vaccine to prevent this horrible disease that kills humans and animals. I have completed every test. I have had success with every animal on which I have tried it. I know it works on animals. But I have never used it on humans. I am afraid to try it."

Mrs. Meister bent over her child and hugged him. She spoke to Pasteur. "Joseph will die if you don't let him have the vaccine. What could be worse than that? You say it works on animals. Perhaps it will work on humans, too. I beg you to try."

"Mr. Pasteur, this is the only hope for Joseph," Doctor Weber said. "If there is a chance that the vaccine will make him better, we must try it."

"Doctor Weber is right," said Mr. Meister. "We are willing to take this chance. Please, we must try the vaccine."

Joseph began to cry in pain. As his mother tried to calm the little boy, Pasteur thought about the doctor's words, "There is a chance that the vaccine will make him better." Without it he would surely die.

I cannot refuse, he thought. I must give Joseph the vaccine.

"Very well," Pasteur said. "We will give him the vaccine. I must not deny him his last chance. He has suffered so much already."

Doctor Weber smiled with relief. "Thank you, Mr. Pasteur. We must pray that the vaccine will cure Joseph as it has cured all the animals which have had it."

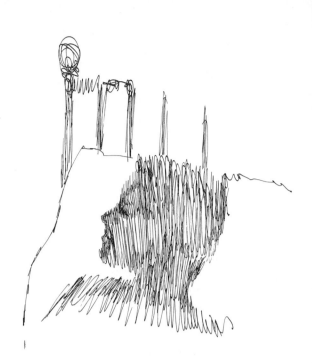

Every day, Joseph was given the vaccine. Each injection was stronger than the last. He received thirteen injections in all. Finally, the night came when he was given the last and strongest injection.

Scarcely sleeping, Pasteur sat at Joseph's bedside all night. He waited and prayed and hoped. He thought, what if the boy dies? What if the vaccine doesn't work on humans?

But it must work! It worked perfectly on animals. There is no reason why it should not work on humans, he argued with himself. If only Joseph can live through this last injection, we will have hope for his recovery.

Louis Pasteur spent an anxious night. In the few moments of sleep that overcame him, he dreamed that the boy died. He awoke terrified. But Joseph was sleeping peacefully. "Thank God," Pasteur whispered as he continued his watch.

The next morning, just as the sun peeked into the window, a sound came from the child on the bed. Pasteur came closer. The child's forehead was cool and his color was good.

"Please, Mr. Pasteur," Joseph said. "I'm hungry. I want my breakfast."

Pasteur smiled for the first time in days. "You shall have it. You shall have your breakfast," he whispered.

The Meisters and Dr. Weber lived in a small region on the French-German border called Alsace-Lorraine. Pasteur's laboratory was in Paris, France. This story took place during the 1880's. Before that time, anyone bitten by a dog with rabies had died. But Joseph Meister lived. From that day on, a way was found to prevent rabies, one of the most dreaded of all diseases.

Louis Pasteur was one of the greatest scientists who ever lived. Through his experiments he helped discover cures for many diseases. He also developed a process for making food safe to eat. This process is called pasteurization. The milk we drink and much of the food we eat today is pasteurized so it will be safe for us.

Louis Pasteur

More To Read

Louis Pasteur, Founder of Bacteriology by John Harvey Mann. Published by Charles Scribner's Sons, New York, 1964.

A DESPERATE

The howling wind swept across the vast ice-covered Arctic. It was bitterly cold, but the men were dressed warmly in furs. The cold was the least of their worries. They were hungry. They were weary. They were discouraged.

Two months earlier the leader of the group, Admiral Robert Peary, had written these words in his diary, "May God help me to seize this great trophy for the Flag."

For as long as Peary could remember he had wanted to fly the Stars and Stripes from the most northerly point in the world and claim it for the United States.

Around him, his little band of Eskimos had waited anxiously. The sledges had been heavily loaded. Even the dogs had seemed eager to start. Twice before, Peary had tried to reach the North Pole, but he had failed each time.

At last Peary had given the signal to start, and they were off. Ahead of them had stretched the jagged ice of the Arctic Ocean.

CHANCE
BY MARIE PEARY STAFFORD

At the end, they had hoped, lay the "great trophy" that they had come to find, the North Pole.

It was in high spirits that the brave little band had left the land behind them and had headed north.

But now, after two months of fighting the cold and the ice, Peary had to make a decision. He looked at the drawn, tired faces of his men. He looked at the pitifully thin dogs and at the small amount of food still left on the sledges. Peary was tempted to go on. But he could not think only of himself. It would not be fair to the others to go on. Even if they were to make it to the Pole, they would never return alive.

Peary made his decision. They would turn back.

They had come nearer to the North Pole than anyone had ever been before. But that was not enough for Peary. To reach the North Pole was the only thing that would satisfy him.

Again he had failed.

167

The problem now was to get back safely.

They were a forlorn little group. The interest and excitement of the outward journey was gone. Disappointment had set in. Their feet dragged. The going was difficult. Each day the wind drove tiny bits of ice and snow into the eyes of the tired men. Night after night, when they made camp, the men were in agony from the burning feeling in their eyes. Only after packing their eyelids with snow until they were numb, did the pain ease enough to let them sleep. Each day they must struggle on again. Each day the food supply grew smaller and smaller. The food was almost gone.

The wind never stopped blowing. The combination of the wind and tide piled up the sea ice in such jagged heaps that the dogs could not drag the sledges over it. Men had to go ahead with pickaxes to make a roadway. This was slow and hard work. The men and dogs grew weaker with every passing day.

At last, with land almost in sight, they received the worst blow of all. After the terrible days of fighting their way across the tumbled ice cakes, they came to a tremendous strip of open water between the fields of ice. This strip of water was called a *lead*. It was two miles wide. Peary had never seen a lead so large. How could they get across?

They made camp on the northern shore. Day after day, they sat there. Day after day they waited, hoping that the winds and tides would move the blocks of ice together again. Each day their food grew less until it was all gone.

Finally, in mercy, they shot the starving dogs. In desperation the hungry men broke up their useless sledges. Using the wood for fuel, they cooked and ate the dog meat. And still the lead was there, two miles of open water between them and the land. It stood between them and any hope of life.

This strip of water was called a lead.

Each day Peary and one of the strongest men in the party walked along the edge of the ice field. One walked toward the east, the other toward the west. They hoped they might find a place where the lead was either closing or showing some sign of freezing over.

One morning the Eskimo who had gone to the east came running back in great excitement. The lead was freezing in one place.

When Peary reached the spot, he realized that it was a desperate chance. But they were desperate men. Their food was gone. Their hope was gone. It was better to take this chance than to die from starvation.

The ice was very thin. But they had to try it. Each man put on his snowshoes, tying them more carefully than he had ever done before.

They started across, keeping their feet far apart, never lifting

them, just sliding them along. Polar bears walk this way on thin ice and the men felt that this would be the safest way. They kept quite a distance apart, in order not to put too much weight on the ice at any one spot.

The ice was so thin that at the toe of each man's snowshoe there was a ripple and a wave. One stumble, one misstep and it would be the end. They shuffled on. Each man was holding his breath. No one dared look to the right or to the left to see how his companions were getting along. It was each man for himself.

When they finally reached the other side, they looked back over the dangerous way they had come. A lane of open water now separated the thin ice. The lead was widening again. They had crossed just in time!

With the big lead at last behind them, they were faced with another problem. And here, for the first time in his experience with them, Peary had trouble with his faithful Eskimos. On land,

171

an Eskimo can find his way anywhere. He never loses his sense of direction. But on the frozen Arctic Ocean there are no landmarks. Peary knew where he was because of his instruments. But the Eskimos did not understand. They knew the sea ice had drifted, but they were sure it had drifted them toward the west where the ship lay. Peary knew that they had drifted east, but the Eskimos would not believe him.

He did not argue or explain. He did not bully them. He did not desert them. Very quietly he said, "We will make camp."

Then, with the last of their fuel, they brewed some tea. As they were drinking, Peary took a gold locket from beneath his fur clothing. He opened it. There were three pictures inside. He showed them one.

"This is my wife," he said. "Do you remember Mrs. Peary?"

Indeed they did. She had always been most kind and friendly.

He showed them the second picture and said, "This is my daughter, Ahnighito. Do you remember the Snowbaby?"

Of course they remembered the Snowbaby. She had played with their children.

Of the third picture he said, "This is my son. You have never seen him. But I can assure you that I am just as anxious to get back to my family as you are to get back to your families. And I promise you that if you will follow me, I will take you the shortest and quickest way to land."

Without another word of argument the Eskimos got up and followed him. He had appealed to their intelligence and to their reason.

They finally reached the coast of Greenland where they found food in abundance. After eating their fill and regaining their strength, the men were soon able to make their way back to the ship and, finally, to their homes.

This adventure took place in 1906. In 1908, Robert Peary went again into the Arctic, and on April 6, 1909, he reached the North Pole. His motto, "I will find a way or make one," had helped him to reach his goal. He had achieved his life's ambition and had added new glory to the flag of his country. Peary had also completely won the loyalty and admiration of the Eskimos. Without them and their dogs he could never have succeeded. He is today a part of their history and folklore. They speak of him as "Pearyoksoah," great Peary of the iron will, who never made a promise that he did not keep, and who never asked a man to do something that he was afraid to do himself. Today, airplanes, tractors, and radios are used by explorers. But Peary had only the combination of man and the Eskimo dog working together.

The author of this story is Admiral Peary's daughter, the Snowbaby, whose picture he carried in his gold locket.

More To Read

The Conquest of the North and South Poles; Adventures of the Peary and Byrd Expeditions by Russell Owen. Published by Random House, New York, 1952.

Peary to the Pole by Walter Lord. Published by Harper & Row, New York, 1963.

The Great

The young Greek boy had just slumped onto his straw bed when the tent flap was lifted and his friend Marcellus entered.

"Pheidippides, I've been looking all over for you!" he cried. "Come and join the victory celebration."

"No, thanks," said Pheidippides. "I'm going to celebrate by taking a nap. I just got back from Sparta. I had to carry a message to our allies."

"Too bad you missed the battle," said Marcellus, nudging his friend. "We couldn't tell which way it would go for awhile. And you should have seen General Miltiades running around like a madman, urging us to fight harder for the glory of Greece." Marcellus laughed as he remembered the general directing the battle.

Marathon Run

By Audrey J. Schuster

"You must have done a pretty good job," said Pheidippides. "I hear the Persians dropped their bows and arrows and ran for their ships."

"That was after they had lost about six thousand men," Marcellus said. "I don't think they'll be bothering the Greeks again."

Suddenly the tent flap was pulled open and a soldier poked his head in.

"What now?" asked Pheidippides sitting up.

"General Miltiades wants to see you," the soldier said. "It sounds like an emergency."

"I thought the emergencies were over when the Persians were defeated," said Marcellus.

"I don't know what it's about," the soldier replied. "But you'd better hurry."

He withdrew his head, and Pheidippides pulled himself to his feet.

"Here I go again," he sighed. He clapped Marcellus on the shoulder and said, "We'll have to celebrate later."

Then he turned and left the tent.

Miltiades was pacing back and forth when Pheidippides entered his tent.

"There you are!" shouted the general, waving his arms. "Come in, come in."

Pheidippides stood at attention as he waited for General Miltiades to stop pacing.

After a few seconds, the general stopped in front of the boy.

"Pheidippides," he said. "I have a most important mission for you. You must go to Athens at once."

"But, sir, I just returned from Sparta," the boy protested.

"Yes, yes, I know," said Miltiades. "But the Persians may be on their way to Athens to attack the city before we can get there. The people of Athens don't know about our victory, and it is possible that they will surrender the city. We must let them know that we have won here at Marathon so that they will hold out until we arrive."

Miltiades stroked his chin thoughtfully. "You are my fastest runner," he declared. "You must take the news to Athens. You are the only one I can trust to reach the city in time."

Pheidippides nodded his head. He was terribly tired. But he realized how important this mission was.

"I understand," he said quietly.

Miltiades smiled. "Good boy, I knew you would do it. Leave at once, and good luck to you!"

Pheidippides saluted and disappeared outside the tent.

The sun was hot and Pheidippides reached for his water flask. Then he remembered he had left it in his tent. He strode back, refilled the flask after taking a deep swallow, and tied it securely to his waist.

Athens was about twenty-five miles away.

Well, at least it's not as far as Sparta, he thought, as he made his way through the camp, pushing between soldiers happy with victory.

He stumbled against a tent peg and barely caught himself

from falling.

"Pheidippides, wait!"

Pheidippides turned and saw Marcellus running toward him.

"Where are you off to now?" asked Marcellus.

"I'm off to Athens," he replied. "Do you want me to give your family any message?"

"No," said Marcellus. "But I'd go slowly if I were you. You look tired."

Pheidippides shrugged, "All in a day's work." He punched his friend playfully in the arm and turned.

"See you soon," he called back.

The army was camped on the slopes of a mountain. Pheidippides decided to climb over the mountain instead of taking the longer route around it. Leaning forward, he lunged up the slopes, side-stepping rocks and weaving between the trees and bushes. At the top of the mountain he stopped to get his breath. Then he plunged down the other side to the road leading to Athens.

Here Pheidippides broke into a trot. He would take Marcellus' advice and go slowly, conserving his strength until he had covered most of the distance. Then he would draw on all his remaining energy to run full speed into the city.

After an hour, sweat was streaming down Pheidippides' forehead, but he had become accustomed to the pace he had set for himself. He was running easily with long, regular strides. He almost forgot how tired he was as puffs of dust kicked up by his heels followed him on the dirt road. He liked to run. It made him feel free and weightless.

He thought of Miltiades. The general had called him his fastest runner. And this was indeed an important mission. The fate of Athens depended on him.

I must get there before the Persians do, Pheidippides thought. Somehow I must run faster.

On he ran as mile after mile passed under his racing feet. Ten miles. Twelve. Fifteen. Could he make it? He was very tired.

Suddenly Pheidippides coughed. A film of dust clung to his skin. Dust had filled his nose and mouth until he could barely breathe. He tried to keep up the pace, but he could not stop coughing.

Gasping, he threw himself to the side of the road under an olive tree. He reached for his flask but realized that water would only make him sick now. He would have to rest first. Soon he was breathing more easily. The shade sent pleasant shivers over his warm body and he began to relax. He removed the flask from his hip, rinsed out his mouth, and then took a few short swallows of the cool water.

Then Pheidippides began to think of his mission again. The entire army was with General Miltiades at Marathon. If the people of Athens thought their army had been destroyed, what would they do? There were few men left to defend the city. Would they surrender to the Persians?

Pheidippides knew he could not afford to rest any longer. The Persian ships might even now be approaching the harbor of Athens. He wiped the sweat from his face and neck. He calculated the distance he had run and decided that he had only about five more miles to go.

The boy stood up and stretched his legs. Slowly, he started off again. His legs were shaky in spite of his rest. But little by little, he increased his speed.

He was almost there. Now was the time for a burst of speed. He stretched his long legs and thrust them out, forcing his body down the road. His arms, raised slightly, pumped back and forth.

He thought that soon he would feel a rush of fresh energy, as he always did when he had been running hard. Instead, energy seemed to be seeping out of his body. With every stride, he felt as if he were moving more slowly. He pushed himself harder.

He had to reach Athens before the Persians did. He kept saying that to himself over and over again.

Ahead he could see the first farms that lay outside Athens. As he drew up to them, several men in the fields raised their heads to stare at him. He raced on.

His heart pounded against his ribs. Trees and fields passed by in a blur. Once he almost went off the road, but he threw himself in the other direction just in time. He opened his mouth wider to suck in air.

He stumbled against some children as he went through the gateway to Athens. He wanted to fall over, to collapse in the street, but his legs carried him on.

Finally, he burst into the center of the market place.

He could hear people murmuring around him and someone touched his arm. Through a blur, he saw one of the rulers of the city.

"Pheidippides, what is it?" cried the man, rushing toward him.

Pheidippides felt his legs give way. He slumped against the ruler. It was impossible to breathe, but he had to give the message. Almost in a whisper, he gasped, "Rejoice! We conquer."

Then he slid to the ground. The ruler bent down and felt the boy's heart. There was no movement. He looked up at the faces of the people crowding around.

"He is dead," the ruler said slowly. "The boy has brought us news of Marathon, and it has cost him his life. Our soldiers have defeated the Persians at Marathon. Thanks to the courage of this young boy, we know of the victory and we will not surrender our city."

"Rejoice! We conquer."
Pheidippides brings news of the victory at Marathon.

A medal of honor
for winners in the
Eighteenth Olympic Games,
Tokyo, Japan, 1964

Pheidippides had arrived in time. The city of Athens was saved from the Persians. The battle of Marathon is one story of a famous battle that supposedly took place about 2,500 years ago. Many of the details of the battle have been handed down to us by word of mouth, so we aren't sure how much of the story is true and how much is legend.

The heroic young messenger, Pheidippides, is remembered in the Olympic games that originated in Greece. The marathon, an endurance race of more than twenty-five miles, is held in honor of his legendary run from Marathon to Athens.

More To Read

Highlights of the Olympics, from Ancient Times to the Present by John Durant. Published by Hastings House, Publishers, Inc., New York, 1961.

181

A NICKNAME THAT STUCK

By Virginia Barrett Novinger

In the early morning hours of June 28, 1778, a quiet had settled over the army camp. Scouts had come in earlier than usual from their rounds and were with General Greene at this very moment.

"What are they talking about?" the soldiers asked each other.

"They're probably planning a big battle."

"If there's much more fighting, we'll all be plumb tuckered out—or dead!"

"What's keeping the scouts in there so long?"

These and other questions remained unanswered until General Greene, himself, came out of his tent.

He told the men that General George Washington had ordered them to attack the British who were camped at Monmouth, New Jersey.

"If you listen, you can hear the rumble of their wagon trains scarcely a stone's throw from here," General Greene said.

Every man was silent. At first, they could hear only the birds chirping in the trees. But then, sure enough, the rumble of wooden wheels disturbing the quiet of the forest proved to the men that the British were, indeed, dangerously near.

It was hot. No breeze stirred. The white undersides of the maple leaves curled over the green topsides in wispy, feathery edgings.

The troops marched to the very edge of the British camp, guns and cannons ready. Soon the battle was raging.

General Greene allowed the men to take off their heavy, woolen uniform coats and fight in their shirt sleeves. Even this really did not lessen their suffering from the heat.

All that day Mary Ludwig Hays, known as Molly to her friends, did what she could for the wounded.

With an old pitcher in hand, she made hundreds of trips to and from the spring carrying water to the men. They would take a quick drink and go back to their guns.

The cries of the men could be heard over the roar of the battle, "Molly, here. Molly, pitcher, pitcher."

And brave Molly carried water and soothed the soldiers as best she could.

Molly's husband, John, was firing a cannon at the front lines.

Just as Molly was hurrying with a drink of water for her husband, she saw him fall at the foot of his cannon. She rushed quickly to his side. She felt his heart and found it was still beating. Molly realized then that he had not been shot, but had fallen from heat exhaustion as so many of the other men had done that day.

A soldier came up on his huge black horse.

"Get this cannon out of the way," he shouted. "There is no one to fire it."

"I'll fire it," Molly cried. "I know how to load it."

The soldier looked at her and rode away.

Molly rammed ammunition into the cannon and continued to pull the pin and fire the weapon all day. Her husband lay at her feet. She poured her last pitcher of water over his hot, burning face. Although she could hear the men crying, "Molly, pitcher, Molly, pitcher," she continued to stay at the cannon, firing round after round of shot.

At last the terrible fighting came to an end. The Americans were victorious!

Not until Molly was quite sure the battle was over did she leave her post at the gun. Then she pulled her husband away from the cannon's base, stretched him under a tree, and went to fetch some cool water for him. Finally, stretcher-bearers came and took John to the hospital.

Then Molly brought water to the other men. Pitcher by pitcher, she carried the precious water so desperately needed by the soldiers.

Near midnight she finally fell asleep.

The next day, the smoke of battle was gone, and the June sun shone again. Molly was surprised to hear General Greene calling her name as he rode through the camp.

"Molly," he said, as he reined in his horse. "General Washington wants to see you." He smiled encouragingly at the brave little woman.

A painting of the Battle of Monmouth by John Ward Dunsmore

185

"But look at me!" she said. "I can't let the general see me looking like this." Her hands flew to her hair, and she looked at her dress, now dirty and torn. The blood of many soldiers was ground into the ragged skirt. The white collar that had long ago disappeared was being used as a bandage for some soldier's wound.

"I just couldn't face General Washington looking this way." Molly turned to go back to her husband.

"Molly," General Greene said, a bit sternly. "General George Washington is not going to see the dirt and grime. He is going to see a brave and wonderful woman. Now, come, you will have time to pretty up later on."

So, Molly went forward to see General George Washington. She was tired, but she stood straight and tall as the general announced that she would be given the rank of sergeant in the United States Army.

"Never have I seen a woman so brave," General Washington said.

A mighty roar from the throats of the thousands of men followed General Washington as he led cheer after cheer for the woman who had helped so courageously.

A tear slid down Molly's cheek.

She thanked the general, curtsied, and then went back to her husband's side.

From that time until the end of the Revolutionary War, Mary Ludwig Hays cared for the wounded men. She brought them water. She bandaged their wounds. She told them stories to make them laugh.

"Come now, soldier, drink from Molly's pitcher! You'll feel better for it," she would say.

"Molly, pitcher, Molly, pitcher," echoed through the hills and valleys in those days. It is sure that when Molly heard her name, she would be there to give comfort to the brave, fighting men.

Mary Ludwig Hays is remembered by the name the soldiers gave her during the hot June days in 1778. We now know her as "Molly Pitcher."

More To Read

Molly Pitcher, Girl Patriot by Augusta Stevenson. Published by
The Bobbs-Merrill Company, Inc., Indianapolis, 1960.

"They Will

By Frances Carpenter

Like a swift arrow, the Indian runner darted from the forest and into the chief's wigwam. He could hardly catch his breath as he fell on one knee before his chief, the great Powhatan.

"News! Big news, O Chief of Chiefs! I bring news of the pale-faced ones!"

The people of the Indian village rushed into the large wigwam to listen. A young girl pushed her way through the crowd. Without fear, she came close to the mighty Indian chief. She was the chief's own daughter.

The girl was anxious to hear the news that the runner brought to her father. She wanted especially to hear about the pale-faced English captain, whom she admired. "Tell your news, man!" the chief ordered.

"The pale-faced captain is our prisoner at last. Our braves are bringing him here to our village."

At these words the Indian girl gasped. She saw the look of joy that came into the fierce eyes of her father. And she was afraid.

"It is good!" said the chief. "When does the prisoner come here?"

Kill You!"

"They march with him close behind me, O Chief of Chiefs. Before the night falls, he can be put to death."

"Yes, the pale-faced one must be killed," the crowd shouted. And then the girl was even more afraid for her friend, the captain.

"We will hold a council to decide whether he will live or die," said the Powhatan.

The girl stood in the very front of the crowd that watched as the prisoner was brought into the chief's wigwam. When the captain gave her a friendly smile, tears came into her eyes. How brave he was!

The Powhatan called the leaders of the tribe together to decide what to do with the captain. Soon they reached a decision. He was to die!

There was a hush in the wigwam when the captain was thrown to the ground at the feet of the chief. Many strong hands held his head down on the flat earth. War clubs were raised, ready to beat the prisoner to death. The chief had only to say the word.

It was then that the chief's daughter

ran out of the crowd. She threw herself down at the side of the captain. With her own body, she shielded his head from the war clubs.

"Spare this man, my father!" she cried. "I claim his life for myself after our custom."

There was silence in the wigwam. But in everyone's mind there was the same thought. The chief's daughter is indeed brave. Who but she would dare speak so boldly to the chief?

The old chief looked at his daughter, and then he spoke. "Put away the war clubs! The man's life shall be spared. My daughter takes him for her brother."

So it was that the English captain was adopted into the tribe. And for a time there was peace between the Indians and the English settlers.

One year went by. And another year came. This second year was a very bad year. There was hunger and cold in the log cabins of the Englishmen. Men fell ill from lack of food. Some died. But still the English settlers stayed in the country of the Powhatan.

"At first I thought the pale-faced ones had come to us only

as visitors," the chief said one day to his daughter. "I thought they would soon go away again. Now I see that they mean to take our land for themselves. They cut our trees for their log houses. They eat our deer and our corn. It is winter. And food is hard to get. Soon we shall be hungry ourselves." The old chief shook his head.

"Now they must go back across the wide waters," he declared. "We shall starve them until they have left our lands."

The girl heard her father send out the order, "Give the pale-faced ones no corn! Give them no deer meat!"

Soon the chief's order was spread to all the Indians in the tribe. And of course, none of the Indians dared to disobey their chief.

Late one afternoon, the English captain and his men brought their small sailing ship up the river to the Powhatan's village. Behind their ship was tied a barge to carry away the corn and the deer meat which the old chief had promised them.

"But I have no corn to give you," the chief said. "There is no deer meat to spare. You say you are hungry. Then go back to your own land."

There was no friendship in the chief's hard voice. The chief's daughter stood at her father's side and was sad at heart when she heard her father speak.

"You promised me food, O Chief of Chiefs," the captain said. "We made a bargain, you and I. You wanted houses of wood. You wanted a rooster, and a hen, and copper, and beads.

"We are building your houses," he went on. "I have brought you what you asked for. I have kept my part of the bargain. Now you must keep yours. I must have food for my people."

At first the great Indian chief shook his head. But he could not go back on his word. After much talk he agreed to send baskets of corn and meat down to the ship.

The girl watched her English brother lead his men toward the river. She saw the braves bring out the baskets of food.

All seemed well now between her father and the captain. But still the girl was uneasy. And fear almost choked her when the chief began to speak to the men gathered around him.

"If we cannot starve the pale-faced ones, we shall have to kill them," he said. "Tonight we shall surprise them. We shall send them a feast in friendship. Then as they eat the feast, we will attack them."

Quietly, the chief's daughter slipped away. No one saw her

creep off into the forest. Her moccasins made no sound as she ran along the snowy trail. She had to warn the captain!

Faster and faster she ran. Like a young deer she made her way through the dark woods.

Black clouds covered the sky. She was glad there was snow on the ground. It helped her to see the dark trunks of the trees.

Twigs scratched the face of the running girl. Her flying, black hair caught on the tree branches. Her headband of precious blue beads was pulled off. But she did not turn back.

I must get there in time, she said to herself. Aloud she cried

out, "Great Spirit up in the Heavens! Let me be in time!"

The darkness did not worry the brave Indian girl. Nor did the noises of the wild beasts make her afraid. An owl screeched, shrill and eerie, just over her head. A fox barked not far away. And once a deer came crashing through the trees.

But she only ran faster. She thought she could already hear the voices of the braves whom her father was sending with the feast.

At last she saw the wigwam in which the captain and his men were staying for the night. With one last great effort she rushed

up to the wigwam, burst through the entrance, and stood there, panting and frightened.

"Little Sister!" the captain cried out. He could not believe what he saw.

The girl was trembling. Her breath came fast. She could scarcely speak.

"O my brother, go quickly! Go away now! The chief will kill you and your men tonight."

"Come, warm yourself, my dear child." The Englishman tried to draw the girl closer to the fire.

"There is no time," she cried. "Already the braves are on their way. They are bringing a feast for you. But it is a trick. While you eat, they will steal your thundersticks and your long knives. Then they will kill you with their war clubs."

"It shall not happen now, my dear sister. You have saved my life a second time. You have warned us in time. We shall be on guard. Our thundersticks will be ready."

Pocahontas, the young Indian girl in this story, not only saved the lives of the captain, whose name was John Smith, and his men, but, in doing so, she also saved the first English settlement in America.

This story took place long before the United States became a nation. The land of the Powhatan was the part of America we know today as Virginia.

Captain John Smith later was wounded in a gunpowder accident and sailed to England, where he recovered. Then he returned to America to explore and settle other colonies.

Pocahontas married an Englishman, John Rolfe, and went to live with him in England. She became ill and died in England at the age of twenty-two.

A painting of Pocahontas

Pocahontas had played an important part in the founding of America.

Frances Carpenter, the author of this story, has written a book about Pocahontas called *Pocahontas and Her World*, published by Alfred A. Knopf, Inc., New York.

More To Read

Pocahontas by Ingri M. and Edgar P. d'Aulaire. Published by Doubleday & Company, Inc., New York, 1946.

"Cut His

Head Off!"

By Eileen Larsen

Marco woke up to the sounds of war. Battle cries and the sound of galloping horses thundered through the thin walls of Marco's tent. For a moment he sat frozen, expecting the armies to crash in upon him.

Where am I? he wondered, looking around the small, cluttered tent. He had been dreaming of his home far away, but the noise had shattered his dream. He remembered that he was in a land called Persia, far from home, on a little hill overlooking a broad green plain.

Cautiously Marco crept to the tent door and lifted the flap. Small bushes screened his view and he could see nothing. Staying close to the ground, he inched forward. And then he saw what was going on!

Below him the wide plain seethed with action. Men on foot swarmed toward each other like troops of ants, in a slow, horrible rhythm of destruction. Around them corps of horsemen charged across the side of the hill and down into the sea of men, meeting other horsemen. The riders, dressed in splendid silks and bright armor, thrust spears at each other, and crossed curving swords that flashed like comets in the sun. Arrows flew up in short arcs and poured down on the troops. And over the whole scene floated clouds of dust stirred up by the galloping horses.

Marco lay motionless, scarcely breathing. The brilliant colors, the tides of movement, the drums and screams and battle cries overwhelmed him. So this was war! His father and his uncle had told him of the fighting they had seen. But even their most vivid words had not prepared him for the horror before him.

His father and his uncle—where were they? Now Marco remembered. They had ridden off last night, and he had promised
to stay and guard the tent and the precious maps inside.

"There's no reason for us all to go so far out of our way just to
buy horses," his father had said. "We can go much faster if we
don't have to bring all our baggage with us. Your uncle and I
should be back by noon."

Marco squinted up at the sky. Noon was not far off.

He inched forward for a better view. It was hard to tell one
side from the other. Each man seemed to have chosen his own
favorite fighting clothes. None of the men wore uniforms. Marco
wondered how the warriors knew who to fight and who to call
comrade. He wondered—

Twanggg! A spear thumped into the ground inches from Marco's face. He looked up in astonishment and saw two horsemen
only a few feet away. As he struggled to his feet, soldiers seized
him from behind.

They pushed him forward toward the two horsemen. "You!" cried the taller of the pair, in the Persian language, "Who are you, and which side are you spying for?"

Marco was glad his father had insisted he study languages. He answered in Persian, "Oh, sir, I am not a spy—"

"I told you so!" said the warrior to his companion, in the Mongolian language. "He speaks Persian. He is a Persian spy. Take him away," he ordered the soldiers. "And behead him."

"Wait!" yelled Marco desperately in Mongolian, as the soldiers started to drag him down the hill. "I am not a spy! I am a traveler!"

The tall man only laughed, but his companion stopped the soldiers. "Release him," he said.

"But colonel—" the tall man protested.

"I am in charge here," said the colonel. "Come here, lad. We might as well hear your story now. You won't be talking much after you are beheaded." He smiled at his own joke.

"I am not a spy," began Marco shakily. "I am a traveler from Venice."

The colonel frowned. It was obvious that he had never heard of Venice.

"I am from Venice, in Italy—in Europe," Marco explained. "And I am traveling with my father and my uncle to see Kublai Khan."

Both horsemen reacted when Marco said the name of their ruler, but not as he had expected. They laughed.

"My boy, you are a good liar, but a liar nevertheless," said the colonel. "Going to see Kublai Khan—why that's as ridiculous as saying you're going to go to the moon! Do you take us for fools? We know that no European has ever gone to see the Khan. You are a spy!"

"Sir," said Marco angrily. "I never lie. My father and my uncle visited Kublai Khan once before. He asked them to stay, but they had business to settle in Venice. And they wanted to bring me back with them. The great Khan let them go, and they promised to return. They are keeping their promise and we are on our way to see the Khan now."

"And just where are these brave and daring men who are such good friends with our ruler?" asked the colonel sarcastically. "Why aren't they here to prove your story?"

"Sir, they went to purchase horses—" Marco began.

"A likely story!" The colonel shook his head. "We might as well proceed with the execution." He motioned to the soldiers. "Cut his head off!"

"Sir, wait!" Marco pleaded. "If I am condemned to die, I have the right to ask one favor of you." Marco held his breath.

"What is the favor?" the colonel demanded.

"Sir, I wish to die right here, at high noon. It is nearly that time now. You'd only have to wait a little while longer."

The colonel hesitated for a moment, and then nodded. "If that is what you wish. A few minutes one way or the other can't matter much." He swung off his horse and walked over to stare down at the raging battle.

Marco sank to his knees. He was too weak to stand. If only my father would return when he said he would, Marco thought desperately. He has the royal seal Kublai Khan gave him. These men must honor that seal. It proves that he is a friend of the Khan's.

But would his father return in time? Marco glanced at the sun. It was nearly overhead and he knew that the time of his execution was only minutes away.

Marco looked out toward the hills from which his father and uncle must come. But he saw no one. He covered his eyes in

despair. If his father did not return quickly, Marco would be put to death.

Suddenly, a cry came from one of the soldiers. Marco looked up and jumped to his feet. Far in the distance, he saw two men leading a string of horses and ponies.

"You see?" Marco shouted. "There is my father!"

"So that's why you wanted to wait," the colonel said. "Smart boy. But all you have done is caught us two more spies."

Swiftly the colonel ordered the soldiers back behind the trees. Each pulled out an arrow and fitted it to his bow. "Don't shoot till they are close enough to kill," he warned them.

One of the soldiers looked worried. "Sir, suppose they really are the Khan's friends," he said. "If we kill them, the Khan will have *us* beheaded."

"True," the colonel agreed. "Hold your fire!"

As the two men rode up to the tent, the soldiers stepped out from behind the trees.

"What is all this?" Marco's father demanded. "What is going on here?"

The colonel stepped forward. "Your son is under arrest for spying," he said. "Have you any way of proving his innocence and your own?"

"Of course," Marco's father replied indignantly. "Would a spy or a spy's father be carrying this?" he asked, holding out the royal seal.

The colonel took the seal carefully and looked at it for a long time. Then he pulled out a red silk scarf and mopped his forehead with it. "We almost made a terrible mistake," he said quietly. Then he bowed. "My deepest apologies, gentlemen, and my profound regrets to you, young man, for the inconvenience we almost caused you."

"Inconvenience?" Marco's father asked with a puzzled expression.

"They were going to cut off my head," explained Marco.

His father nodded gravely. "That *would* have been an inconvenience," he agreed.

Marco, the boy in this story, was Marco Polo. With his father
and his uncle, he traveled from Venice, Italy, to China about
seven hundred years ago. They remained in China as honored
members of Kublai Khan's court for many years. And when at
last they returned to Venice, they had seen more of China and
the Far East than any other Europeans. There are many things
we don't know about Marco Polo. We don't know whether the
events in this story happened exactly as they are told here. But
they could have.

Marco Polo wrote a book telling about the strange and exciting things he saw. But most of the people who read it laughed at
the stories. They thought that surely such people, such places,
and such wealth as Marco described, existed only in dreams!

But one boy who read Marco Polo's tales believed them. And
he tried to reach the fabled land of China in his own way. But
instead of reaching China he found another wonderful place,
America. His name was Christopher Columbus.

More To Read

They Put Out to Sea; the Story of the Map by Roger Duvoisin. Published by Alfred A. Knopf, Inc., New York, 1943.

Adventures and Discoveries of Marco Polo by Richard J. Walsh. Published by Random House, New York, 1953.

World of Marco Polo by Walter Buehr. Published by G. P. Putnam's Sons, New York, 1961.

"خیر آقا ، مَن جاسوس نیستم"

"Oh, sir, I am not a spy—"

These are the words Marco spoke in the Persian language when the soldiers discovered him. They are written above in Persian.

WANTED:
young skinny wiry fellows

Fire!

A wall of flames spread across the horizon in front of the young rider and his pony.

The flames made the pony whinny with fear. Billy patted her neck, whispered, "Easy does it, girl," and jumped from the saddle. He held the pony's head against his shoulder and tickled her nose while he tried to think of a way to get through the fire.

By Robert West Howard

Billy knew he couldn't turn back. He dismissed the thought with an angry shake of his head. There were too many people depending on him. Across the desert other mail boys were waiting for their turn to carry the leather mail pouches. And it was up to Billy to carry the mail the first fifty miles from St. Joseph, Missouri, to the Seneca Station in Kansas.

Billy stared at the wall of flames and then at the dark clouds around the red sun. In those clouds could be rain and howling winds—perhaps even a tornado. A few hours from now a storm might put out the prairie fire. But Billy couldn't wait. He had to get through now! But how? He glanced from side to side trying to find an answer.

A half mile to his right, a line of bushes and cottonwood trees ran straight through the fire. Of course! He'd forgotten for the moment. There was a creek there! He could get through the flames by leading the pony through the creek. It might be a little warm, but they would be safe from the fire. Getting the leather mail pouches wet didn't matter. That storm would break loose with a lot more water before he could get to the Seneca Station.

It seemed strange that a fire so big should be roaring over the prairies this early in the spring! Someone may have left a campfire smoldering . . .

Then Billy remembered something. Back in St. Joseph when he started his ride, he had noticed a half-dozen Indians standing along the railroad station wall. Their black eyes took in everything. This could be an Indian trap. The fire could have been started by Indians to make him ride over to the creek. They might be waiting there to kill him. But that was the only way through the fire!

Billy slipped his revolver out of its holster, checked the bullets, and cocked the trigger. Then he tucked it back into the holster.

Even if there weren't any Indians, there was still the fire. His plan was to ride over to the bushes, blindfold the pony with his shirt, and lead her through the creek. As long as she didn't see the flames, she would be all right.

Billy mounted and turned the pony toward the line of bushes. The frightened pony reared and galloped off at full speed. Billy eased his body forward along her neck, the way Indians ride.

His right hand lay against his gun, ready to whip it out at the first sign of trouble.

He reined to a stop as he reached the edge of the bushes. He remained perfectly still and listened. There was something moving in the bushes!

Billy's fingers closed around the gun. He walked the pony slowly through the bushes toward the creek.

Suddenly, a howling sound split the air and something crashed through the bushes behind him. Billy whipped out his gun and whirled around in the saddle.

It was a coyote! The pony must have frightened it!

Billy sighed with relief. He edged the pony down the bank of the creek and into the water.

He rode out to midstream. So far the water was only three feet deep. They should be able to make it without swimming. And there were no signs of Indians yet. He scrambled off the pony's back and into the water.

Dusk was rolling in. The shadows of the boulders and earth banks blended into the gray water. The smoke made his eyes smart and his throat tickle. Gun in hand, he led the pony up the creek toward the flames. The pony tugged back on the rein and whinnied. That did it! If there were any Indian ponies around, they would whinny back. He stood perfectly still.

Upstream something splashed and came leaping toward them. He held the gun ready to fire until he saw the shadow fill out to two deer and a fawn, running toward safety.

From the top of the bank he heard an owl hoot. After an instant of silence another hoot came from behind them. Indians often signaled to one another with birdcalls and animal cries. Billy crouched against the pony's legs, studying the bank of flame just ahead for any tall shadows that could be Indians. The first owl hooted again. Then he could see its eyes, two bright twinkles reflecting the flames as the owl flapped up from a cottonwood tree and soared away to its mate.

Caressing the pony's trembling nose, Billy slipped off his shirt. He dropped it over the pony's head and tied the sleeves loosely beneath her jaws.

Funny thing about horses, Billy thought, they go berserk in a

fire. But blindfolded and led by someone they trust, they will follow almost as gently as puppies.

The pony pranced and tugged back as she came close to the searing heat. "Easy," Billy whispered. "Another couple of minutes and we'll be safe."

They were surrounded by flames now. Both sides of the creek bank were ablaze. The smoke blinded him. He staggered straight ahead at a run, one arm out.

The words of that advertisement he had first read in the St. Joseph newspaper two months before raced through his mind.

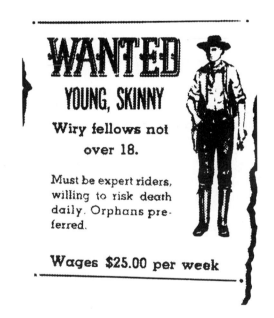

WANTED
YOUNG, SKINNY

Wiry fellows not over 18.

Must be expert riders, willing to risk death daily. Orphans preferred.

Wages $25.00 per week

Well, this was only the first 50 miles! Out there in the Rocky Mountains and the scorching desert the other fellows would have real trouble. They wouldn't get scared and choked up about some little thing like a prairie fire. They would have to face Indians and blizzards, deserts and grizzly bears, avalanches and floods.

Billy was almost through the flames now. He could see safety just ahead. But the smoke was filling his nostrils. He was getting dizzy. He seemed to be falling into a tunnel, down and down, with his lungs on fire.

Billy woke and found himself sprawled on the creek bank, the cool water sloshing across his shoulders, the pony nuzzling his neck. The flames crackled several yards behind them. The air was sweet and clean. He sucked it in, stood up, and shook himself. There had been no Indians.

He had made it!

The pony had worked the shirt most of the way off, nudging him. Billy tossed it back across the saddle and led her up the bank.

The western sky spit lightning. The thunder muttered like a hundred bulls bellowing a long way off. His hands felt carefully down the leather blanket and across each mail pouch. Everything seemed to be in good shape.

"Let's go," he whispered and squished back into the saddle. "We're going to be about an hour late, I reckon."

Billy Richardson, the young man in the story, was one of the first pony express riders. His ride took place in April, 1860.

For the next year and a half, the pony express riders carried the mail from St. Joseph, Missouri, to San Francisco, California. The last pony express ride was made in October, 1861. After that, messages could be sent across the "great desert" by telegraph wire faster than by pony express.

On his first ride, Billy Richardson arrived at the station in Seneca, Kansas, an hour and a half late, slowed by the storm. Billy passed the mailbags along to Jim Beatley, who raced west on his fifty-mile run. The mail arrived in San Francisco ten days later.

More To Read

The Pony Express by Samuel Hopkins Adams. Published by Random House, New York, 1950.

Riders of the Pony Express by Ralph Moody. Published by Houghton Mifflin Co., Boston, 1958.

The Daring One-Armed Major

By Anne Merriman Peck

"I don't aim to get drowned in this canyon," growled Dunn.

The other men stared at him in dismay. Dunn was a trapper with lots of experience in wilderness country. If he was afraid, they were really in danger!

"I've never seen such waterfalls," Howland spoke up. "The whole river drops about twenty feet over the rocks. Then there are more falls and more rapids. You can't even see the river beyond the falls."

"Men, we set out to explore the Colorado canyons, all the way to the end," the one-armed major said. "Come now, don't let bad waterfalls scare you. We've had some narrow escapes before on this trip. Maybe this will be our last battle with the river."

The other men were too tired and discouraged to speak. They were trapped between the huge black walls of the canyon that towered several hundred feet above their heads. The river rushed between the cliffs with the speed of an express train. The roar of the rushing water echoed from wall to wall.

For three months these men had struggled through miles and miles of canyons. They had fought the river at its worst in the great gorges now called the Grand Canyon. Their boats had been overturned, beaten on rocks, and nearly smashed. Many times they had barely

escaped drowning. Now, when they listened to the terrifying roar of water ahead, their courage gave out.

"Major," shouted Howland above the noise of the water. "We'll never live through those falls. The boats will be smashed. We'll have to get out of the canyon some other way."

He turned and pointed to the towering walls, "There are some breaks and ridges in the cliffs. We could climb there and try to reach the top. It's not so dangerous as the river."

The major stood up and smiled at his comrades. The very sight of him gave them courage. This man had brought them through many tight spots, and they trusted him.

"Sure we're all tired and hungry," he

said. "There isn't much food left. But we have come through some mighty rough water. And we're still alive. I figure we're almost through the canyons. How can we give up now? I'm going on. I hope you will come with me!"

The major turned and walked along the shore while the other men argued among themselves.

"Look here, we can't desert the major," said Bradley, a young man who had been with the major in the army. "He's brought us through the worst of scrapes. Even though he has only one arm, he always takes on the hardest jobs himself."

"But we'll die if we take the boats over those falls," argued Howland. "Our only chance is to climb the cliffs and get out of this canyon."

Howland's brother agreed.

"I'll stick with the major," Bradley said.

"Count me in on that. I'm going all the way with the major," one of the other men said.

"Well, I'm going with the Howlands," Dunn said. "I'm not going to take a chance on those falls."

The other men decided to stay with the major.

When the major returned, Howland spoke first. "It's hopeless, major. We'll never get out of here alive. I'm leaving."

"Is that the decision of the group?" asked the major quietly.

The Howland brothers and Dunn nodded.

Bradley spoke for the others. "Major, the rest of us will stick it out with you to the end."

They decided to separate, but there was sadness in their hearts. They felt that they might never see each other again.

In the morning the Howland brothers and Dunn said good-by to their companions. They started the climb, from boulder to ledge, up the face of the canyon wall.

The other men turned to the boats. With their companions gone there were not enough men to handle three boats, so one boat was left behind.

"Let's go, men!" commanded the major. "No sense putting it off any longer."

As soon as the boats hit the swift current, they were swept downstream until the men steered them to a strip of shore near the falls. The waves breaking over rocks, the clouds of spray, and the thunder of water as the river rushed over the brink of the falls brought fear to every heart.

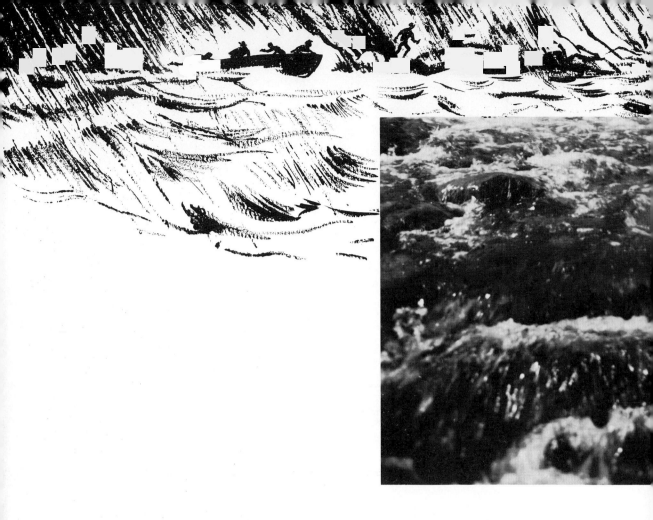

The major planned to launch one boat with a long, strong rope tied to it. They would try to hold back the speed of the boat by hanging on to the rope with all their strength, while they clung to boulders on the shore. They would try this boat over the falls first.

"Major, let me go with the boat," Bradley volunteered. "If the rope breaks, we'll lose the boat unless there's someone to steer it out of the rapids."

Before the major could answer, Bradley stepped into the boat and pushed it out from shore. The waves seized it, tossed it back against the cliffs, tossed it out again into the river, and dashed it against rocks. The men held tight to the rope, but the pull of the speeding boat was too powerful. The rope slipped from their hands!

Horrified, they saw the boat go sweeping over the brink of the falls. It disappeared in the waves and spray. What would hap-

pen to Bradley? Would he be crushed to death on the rocks?

At last, the anxious watchers saw Bradley tossing in the rapids below the falls. The boat was speeding ahead of him. While they watched, Bradley went under, then came to the surface again and fought the waves. He managed to reach the overturned boat and cling to it while he pushed it, bit by bit, out of the swift current to a cove of quiet water. Then he climbed into the boat and waved to his companions. But he was still in danger of being swept into a whirlpool.

"Come on, men, he's still in trouble," the major shouted. "We've got to get to him."

The major sent two men scampering over the cliffs.

The rest of the men climbed into the other boat and shoved it away from shore. At once they were sped toward the falls. Over the brink they went! They were thrown out of the boat. Down, down they sank, under torrents of water. Gasping for breath,

they struggled to the surface. Powerful waves swept over them, sucked them under, and rolled them over and over.

The men fought for their lives among the cruel rocks and smothering water. They swam when they could as the water swept them on and on. When the waves became less furious, they struggled ahead until they caught the boat. Slowly, they pushed it into the cove where Bradley was waiting on the shore, shouting and waving his arms. With Bradley's help, the battered men crawled out of the water. Soon the two who had gone over the cliffs joined them.

These tough men were not ashamed to hug each other. They were so glad to be alive! The major shook the water out of his hair and eyes like a wet dog.

"We're here, men, alive and safe," he gasped. "We've done it —we are the first men to come through the Colorado River canyons!"

The one-armed major in this story was John Wesley Powell. Major Powell and his companions made the first journey through the hundreds of miles of Colorado River canyons in 1869. The brave adventurers continued downstream after they conquered the falls until they came to a settlement. There they were welcomed heartily. No one had expected to see them alive. The three men who had left the party to climb the canyon wall reached the top, but they had soon been killed by Indians.

Nowadays, skilled rivermen with special boats take parties through some of the Colorado canyons.

More To Read

First Through the Grand Canyon by Steve Frazee. Published by Holt, Rinehart & Winston, Inc., New York, 1960.

Down the Colorado with Major Powell by James Ramsey Ullman. Published by Houghton Mifflin Co., Boston, 1960.

Major John Wesley Powell

CHASED BY MOHAWK WARRIORS!

By William F. Keefe

It was early morning. A young Indian warrior came out of his lodge in the Mohawk village. He wore only moccasins and deerskin breeches. In his hand, he carried a hatchet. A knife hung from his belt.

"Orimha!" called one of the women. "Where are you going?"

The young warrior stopped. "To cut wood, mother," he answered.

The woman smiled, and Orimha walked toward the forest. But he was not thinking of his work. Today, I will return to my own people, he thought. He whispered his real name, his French name, Pierre. But the French word sounded strange. He had lived with the Mohawks for nearly two years.

Walking to the edge of the forest, he started cutting some branches. No one must know he was running away. Little by little, he moved into the thick forest.

After a while Orimha looked back. He was deep in the forest. He could no longer see the lodges or the women. He could no longer see the smoke rising from the fires.

Orimha dropped the sticks and the hatchet he was carrying and began to run. He had been well trained by the Mohawks. He could run as long and as fast as any Indian.

222

The sun rose higher, but the day was cool. Brambles and thorns tore at Orimha's bare shoulders and chest. Branches cut him. But he kept on. Many miles ahead was the village of Fort Orange. That was where he would be safe.

Once before Orimha had tried to escape from the Mohawks. But he had been caught.

This time, if the Mohawk warriors caught him, they would probably kill him. The Mohawks were at war with the French. The Mohawk chief had not returned from the battles. He had been gone for many weeks. If the old chief had been killed by the French, there was no chance that Orimha would be spared. He would be killed because his people had killed the chief.

All through the day he ran across glades and over hills. He was far from the Mohawk village now. But he would not be safe until he reached Fort Orange.

Night fell. Orimha knew a trail that led to Fort Orange. But he was afraid that he would meet some of the Mohawks if he followed the trail. He couldn't take the chance of being captured again. So he ran through a part of the forest where there were no paths.

Rabbits and other small creatures dashed away as the youth passed. Orimha splashed and swam across rivers and creeks. The cold water took his breath away. His feet broke the thin ice that had formed along the banks of the rivers.

Dawn made the sky bright at last. Orimha began to feel weak. He had been running a whole day and a night. He had not eaten since he had left the Indian village. He wanted to lie down, to sleep. He needed food. But he couldn't stop. The warriors were probably out looking for him already. And they would know that he was heading for Fort Orange.

Everywhere he looked in the forest, he seemed to see the faces of the warriors! He thought he saw them peering through the bushes and trees. But he ran on.

Again it was afternoon, and the sun began to settle slowly in the western sky. As the shadows of afternoon grew long, Orimha saw smoke. The smoke was coming from the chimney of a small cabin.

Orimha stopped. Moving from bush to bush, he crept closer to the cabin. A settler was cutting firewood nearby. When Orimha was very close, he called out in a friendly way. "I greet you," he said in the language spoken by the Mohawks.

At once the settler came toward him. "Let us be friends," Orimha said.

The settler smiled. He took Orimha into his cabin, and his wife fed the young boy. For the first time in many hours Orimha ate.

The settler agreed to take a message to Fort Orange. This was Orimha's best chance. The Mohawks wouldn't stop the settler. And now Orimha could rest in the safety of the settler's cabin until help came from the fort.

Orimha relaxed on a cot. He was very tired after his long journey, and soon he was sound asleep.

Suddenly he was awakened by someone shaking him. It was the settler's wife. "Mohawk warriors!" she cried. "They are coming this way."

Orimha rushed to a window. He saw a searching party of Mohawk warriors coming toward the cabin. It was too late to get away.

"Quickly!" the settler's wife urged. "Follow me!"

She led him to a corner of the room and hid him under a pile of sacks in the corner.

He heard voices outside the cabin. They must be searching for him!

They were coming closer!

Orimha held his breath and remained perfectly still. If the Indians were to find him, they would kill both him and the settler's wife.

After a long agonizing moment, the voices moved away. Then they were gone.

At last the settler's wife said, "It is safe now!"

Orimha thanked her and went back to the cot. But he was wide awake now. He couldn't sleep. He lay there resting, waiting for the settler to return.

Suddenly, he heard voices from outside. He rushed to the window and looked out. It was too dark. All he could see were four shadowy figures walking toward the cabin. It must be the warriors returning. He thought, this time they will find me.

He hurried back to the corner of the room, and buried himself under the sacks once more.

He heard voices in the cabin. He heard footsteps on the cabin floor. They came straight toward him.

Then someone began pulling the sacks from the pile under which he was hidden.

I am caught, he thought.

Orimha leaped from under the sacks, his knife ready. He would not be captured without a fight. He lunged toward the figure who stood before him. Then he stopped short. It was the settler! Behind him were three men from the fort. They had come to take Orimha back with them.

Orimha had escaped at last.

The real name of Orimha, the young boy in the story, was Pierre Esprit Radisson. He became a famous French explorer and fur trader.

This story took place over three hundred years ago in what is now New York State. Pierre Radisson was born in France. He came to Canada at the age of sixteen and was soon captured by the Indians. After his escape, Pierre explored the North American continent. He is believed to be the first white man to reach the Mississippi River and to explore the great northwest of North America.

In spite of his troubles with the Indians, Pierre never forgot the kindness of his Indian parents. Writing about his travels years later, he said, "I loved those people well."

More To Read

Bay of the North by Ronald Syme. Published by William Morrow & Co., Inc., New York, 1950.

THE RIDE THAT

A door opened and a man slipped quietly out into the dark streets of Boston. He did not notice that his dog, Spot, had come out behind him and was following him.

The streets were filled with red-coated British soldiers. There were sounds of shouted orders and the clank of muskets. In the confusion, none of the soldiers stopped the man who walked with a dog at his heels. He made his way safely through town toward the water front to the house of his friend, Joshua.

"Joshua," he said when his friend greeted him at the door. "I need your help. The British soldiers are getting ready to attack. They're all over town already. I've warned our friends across the river to be ready.

MADE HISTORY

By Clare Thorne

But I must get word to Sam Adams and John Hancock who are hiding in Lexington."

Joshua whistled softly in surprise. "Paul," he said, "If Adams and Hancock are captured by the British, they will be sent back to England and hanged as traitors."

Paul replied, "That's right. You've got to row me across the river. I'll get a horse there and ride to Lexington to warn them."

"I'll row you across," said Joshua. "But we'd better hurry before the moon rises. There is a British ship blocking the river, and if they see us, we'll be done for."

"Let's be quick then! The moon will be up soon."

"I'll get some flannel to wrap the

231

oarlocks so they won't creak," Joshua said. "Wait for me by the boat. And you'd better take off your spurs. They might clink and arouse suspicion."

"My spurs!" Paul exclaimed. "I've forgotten them." How could he ride without his spurs when life and death would hang on his ability to get away from anyone who tried to stop him? And he would be riding a strange horse, too! He couldn't take the risk. But how could he get his spurs? It was too late to go back to the house for them. And he might not be able to get through Boston without being stopped this time. As he stood there, frowning, two little paws pushed against his knee.

"Spot! What are you doing here?" he asked. Suddenly, Paul had an idea. Spot could run faster than a man could walk. And he could get past the soldiers with no trouble. Paul scribbled a note, tied it to Spot's collar, and spoke to the little dog.

"Go straight home, Spot. Give the family this message. And come right back here with my spurs. Mind now! No stopping along the way."

The little messenger wagged his tail and was gone.

By the time Joshua had the boat ready, Spot was back. And he had done his errand. The spurs were tied securely, one to each side of his collar. Paul untied the spurs and sent Spot home again, this time to stay.

The small rowboat moved silently over the water. Paul and Joshua held their breath as the boat eased past the great black hull of the British ship. They saw the cannons that could blow the rowboat to matchsticks. They knew that the British captain had orders not to let any boat cross the river.

The moon was rising, but it was too late to do any harm. As the first long beams made streaks across the water, they reached the other side of the river without being seen.

Minutes later Paul was saddling a horse that had been given to him by one of his friends.

"It's eleven o'clock now," Paul said. "I ought to be in Lexington by midnight if this horse is as good as you say it is!"

He mounted the horse, waved good-by, and was off.

Paul rode faster and faster as he and the small strong horse became used to each other. Each time he passed a farmhouse or a village he shouted the warning, "The Regulars are out! The British are coming!"

In these houses, muskets would be pulled from under mattresses, powder horns and shot pouches filled, and horses saddled in the barn. Soon there would be dozens, perhaps hundreds of men on their way to Lexington.

Paul rode at full speed into the village of Medford. There were many people to warn here. Paul raced through the town shouting to wake the people, "The Regulars are out! The British are coming!"

Without stopping, he left Medford and continued up the road.

Now he was only a mile from the outskirts of Lexington. He would ride straight to the place where Adams and Hancock were hiding. He would warn them and go on to warn the people of Concord . . .

Suddenly, Paul saw two British officers, mounted and waiting in the shadow of an oak tree beside the road. He was so close he could see the pistols in their holsters.

They had already spotted him. One of the officers was turning his horse toward the oncoming rider. The other was starting the other way, to be ready to trap Paul if he escaped the first officer.

Paul moved the reins across his horse's neck.

"Don't fail us now!" he whispered.

The horse turned without slowing, jumped a low stone fence, and raced out across the pasture on the other side. Paul bent low over its neck like an Indian, expecting at any moment to hear the sound of a pistol shot at his back.

Behind him the heavy British horses were getting off to a slow start. The first had just leaped the fence and was starting up the slope of the pasture. Paul spurred his horse up over the top of the rise and started down the other side. Ahead he could see a small woodland where he could lose the officers, if only he could reach it.

He had a hundred yards start—perhaps a little more than that now. But it was not enough for safety.

He swerved his horse just in time to avoid a puddle of clay at the foot of the hill. He almost hadn't seen it! The soft clay would have slowed him down enough for the British officers to catch up with him.

This was his chance to escape! If only the British soldiers wouldn't notice the puddle . . .

As he rode toward the woods, he could hear the thunder of heavy hoofs as the first of the officers started down the slope.

Paul looked back over his shoulder. Yes! The red-coated officer was riding straight for the clay! A moment later the British horse was floundering in the clay puddle.

Paul chuckled into his horse's ear as they rode into the safety of the woods.

Minutes later he was in Lexington, reining his horse in front of the place where Adams and Hancock were hiding.

As he ran toward the door, two men, with muskets raised, stopped him.

"Halt!" they ordered.

"I must see Sam Adams and John Hancock!" Paul cried out.

The men said nothing.

Paul became alarmed. Was something wrong? Had Adams and Hancock been captured by the British? Had he failed in his mission? Who were these men who stood in his way? Then he realized why the men had not answered him. This hiding place had been a carefully guarded secret. For all these men knew, Paul could be a British spy. The men would not admit that Adams and Hancock were inside.

Quickly, Paul told them his name. Upon hearing it, the guards relaxed and lowered their muskets. They knew he was a friend.

"Warn Adams and Hancock!" Paul shouted. "The Regulars are out! The British are coming!"

At once the two men rushed inside with the message. Paul's mission had been successful. Adams and Hancock were warned

But Paul was gone already. He was riding toward Concord— riding to rouse the men who would, tomorrow morning, fire the shots that would be "heard around the world!" He was riding to wake a new nation to life!

Paul Revere

The gallant rider in this story was Paul Revere, one of America's first patriots. Paul Revere's ride has become an American legend. Henry Wadsworth Longfellow wrote a poem about it called, "The Midnight Ride of Paul Revere."

His ride took place the night before the British attacked to start the Revolutionary War. But the Americans were prepared, thanks to Paul Revere.

This ride was not the only contribution Paul made to his country. He also took part in the famous Boston Tea Party in 1773. He was a lieutenant colonel in the Revolutionary Army during the war. When he was not serving his country, Paul was a silversmith.

In spite of all the things Paul Revere did for his country, he is best remembered for an event that lasted for perhaps a single hour on the night of April 18, 1775—his famous ride from Boston to Lexington, Massachusetts.

More To Read

America's Paul Revere by Esther Forbes. Published by Houghton Mifflin Co., Boston, 1946.

Paul Revere and the Minute Men by Dorothy Canfield Fisher. Published by Random House, New York, 1950.

"WE NEED YOU NOW!"

BY WILLIAM F. KEEFE

Jackie watched as thousands of people walked to their seats in the great baseball stadium. Many of the seats were already filled. The sound of music came across the field.

Another ballplayer stood next to Jackie. He slapped his hand into his glove. "You've got to win for us today, Jackie," he said.

239

Jackie looked at his friend Pee Wee in surprise. He wanted to ask Pee Wee what he meant. But the manager of the Brooklyn Dodgers began to talk. Jackie and Pee Wee and the other players gathered around him.

"I don't have to tell you men what this game means to us," the manager said. "If we beat the Phillies today, we're sure of at least a tie for the championship. If we lose, there is a good chance that the season will be over for us."

This was the last game of the season. The Dodgers were tied for first place with the New York Giants. If both the Giants and the Dodgers won their games today, or if they both lost, the season would end in a tie. But if one of them won while the other team lost, the season would be over for the team that lost.

In the grandstands around the field, people began to shout. Their shouting grew to a roar. Jackie, looking across the field, saw the umpire waving.

"Play ball!" the umpire shouted.

"All right, men, here we go!" the manager said.

The game began. Jackie had a chance to bat in the first inning. But he did not get a hit. He came back to the dugout where the other Dodgers were. "What did you mean when you said I had to win this game?" he asked Pee Wee.

"I mean you're our best player, Jackie. You've got to lead us."

Jackie smiled, "I'll do my best, Pee Wee," he said.

Jackie listened to the crowd. Many people were cheering for the Phillies. The game was in Philadelphia, and the people wanted their own team to win.

The Phillies played well at the beginning. Soon, they were leading the Dodgers by four runs. The score was six to two. Jackie was worried. It looked as if the Dodgers might lose.

The scoreboard showed that the Giants were winning their game.

In the fifth inning, Jackie had a turn at bat. He picked up his favorite bat. He gripped it tightly. His hands were sweating because he was nervous.

He stood at the plate and looked down to first base. One of his teammates stood on first.

The Phillies' pitcher threw the ball. Jackie swung and felt the bat hit the ball. The ball sailed far out between the Phillies' left fielder and center fielder. Jackie ran all the way to third base with a triple. The Dodger player who had been on first base scored easily. Before the inning was over, the Dodgers had scored three runs. Now the Phillies were ahead by only one.

But when the Phillies came to bat, they got two more runs. The score was now eight to five in favor of the Phillies.

Just then a roar swept through the crowd. Jackie glanced up at the scoreboard. The Giants had won! Now the Dodgers had to win or the season would be over for them.

The Dodgers couldn't score in the next two innings. But in the eighth inning they scored three runs. The score was tied! Now they had a chance to win the game.

The score was still tied at the end of nine innings. This would be an extra-inning ball game.

It was the twelfth inning! The Phillies had runners on first, second, and third with two out. If the Phillies scored a run, they would win the game.

Jackie stood tensely at his position between first and second base. He watched as the Dodger pitcher threw the ball.

The batter swung hard. The ball cracked against the bat and shot toward second base. Everyone in the stadium jumped to his feet.

Jackie ran desperately to his right. He knew he had to catch this ball or the Dodgers would lose the game. Just when the ball was about to go by him, he leaped into the air. His left hand, with the glove on it, was stretched out as far as it could stretch. While Jackie was still in the air, he felt the ball smack into his glove. He fell to the ground. The whole weight of his body crashed down on his right arm. His elbow smashed into his stomach.

He lay motionless on the ground, but the ball was still in his glove. The inning was over. The Phillies had not been able to score.

Jackie's teammates came running over and helped him off the field. Jackie lay down in the Dodgers' dugout. His right arm, his stomach, and his right side hurt him terribly. He could hardly breathe.

The Dodgers could not score. When the Phillies came to bat again, the Dodgers ran out on the field—all except Jackie. Jackie lay on the bench, his face twisted with pain. Pee Wee came back into the dugout.

"Let's go, Jackie," Pee Wee said. "We need you now. We've never needed you more. You'll be all right as soon as you get out on the field."

Jackie said, "I'm not sure I can help the team, Pee Wee."

"Remember what I told you?" Pee Wee said. "If you can't help, no one can."

Jackie struggled to his feet. Pee Wee helped him. Jackie put on his glove and went back on the field.

The Phillies could not score a run in the thirteenth inning. Then the Dodgers came to bat in the fourteenth inning. The first two men made outs. Now it was Jackie's turn to bat.

Jackie carefully rubbed dust on his hands so he could hold the bat better. He felt tired. His side and his right arm still hurt. He could see the numbers on the scoreboard. They showed that the score was still Phillies eight, Dodgers eight.

The people in the stadium were silent as Jackie stepped to the plate. Everyone watched him.

Jackie felt all alone. He watched the Phillies' pitcher. The pitcher raised his arms and threw. With all his muscles tense, Jackie watched the ball. He swung with all his strength as the ball crossed the plate. The bat met the ball with a loud crack.

Out, out the ball sailed—out toward left field and over the left field wall for a home run. Jackie ran around the bases while the great crowd roared. Jackie's teammates shook his hands as he crossed the plate. The score was nine to eight! The Dodgers were ahead at last!

Jackie ran to the dugout. Pee Wee met him there. Both men were laughing. Pee Wee threw his arm around Jackie's shoulders.

"You did it, Jackie!" Pee Wee shouted. "Now we'll win!"

Jackie in this story was Jackie Robinson, a great baseball player. His friend, Pee Wee, was shortstop Pee Wee Reese, another famous Dodger.

Jackie's home run in the last game of the 1951 baseball season won the game for the Dodgers. And even though the Dodgers lost the championship playoff to the New York Giants, Jackie Robinson's home run is remembered as a great moment in baseball history.

Before he came to the Brooklyn Dodgers, Jackie had become famous in college for his skill at baseball, basketball, football, and track. When he joined the Brooklyn Dodgers in 1947, he became the first Negro to play in the major leagues. He spent ten years with the Dodgers and helped them win National League championships in all but four of those years.

In 1962, Jackie Robinson was elected to the National Baseball Hall of Fame, an honor given only to the greatest baseball players.

More To Read

Famous American Negroes by Langston Hughes. Published by Dodd, Mead & Company, New York, 1954.

Breakthrough to the Big League; The Story of Jackie Robinson by Jackie Robinson and Alfred Duckett. Published by Harper & Row, New York, 1965.

A STEER GONE WILD

By Robert West Howard

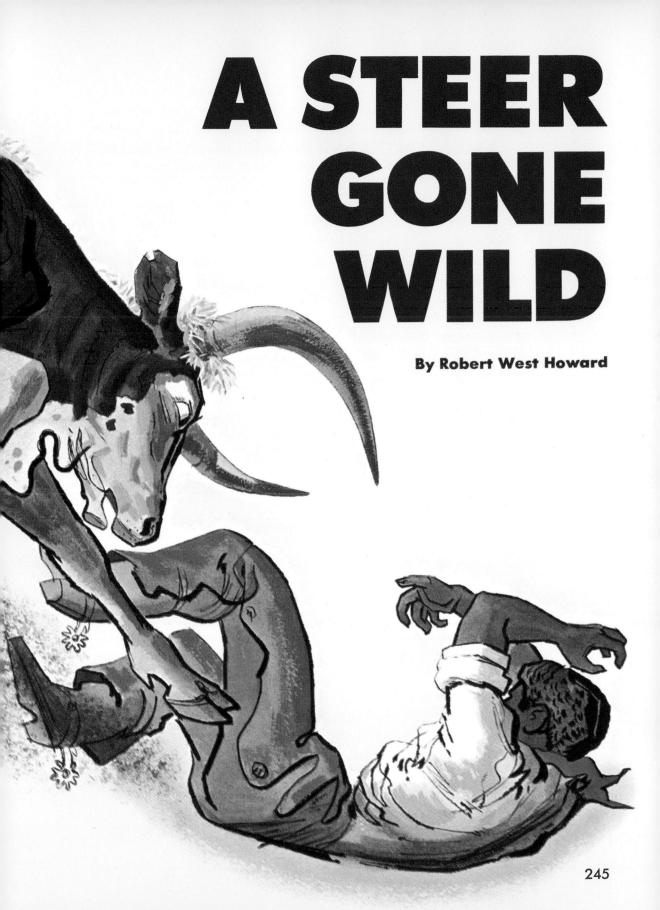

The skinny youngster looked into the arena from behind the grandstand, licked his lips, and groaned. He was scared. He had felt scared ever since that huge rodeo crowd out there began roaring during the entry parade an hour before. Now he and Bill Pickett and some ornery old longhorn steer were due to go out into the arena any minute.

He was afraid that he would get out in front of that crowd and freeze up. If he did, Bill Pickett might get hurt. No, sir. Best thing for him to do was to look for the general manager of the rodeo and tell him to get an older, more experienced cowboy to work with Bill Pickett.

He walked his pony through the sawdust behind the grandstand looking for the general manager.

At last he saw the man. Reining his pony to a stop, he licked his lips and opened his mouth to speak.

But the general manager spoke first. "You all ready to go, Will?"

"Well—" The youngster just sat there. He couldn't get the words out.

The general manager walked over to him and spoke softly. "Son," he said. "Every man here is just as scared as you are. I am, too. But Pickett is counting on you. I'm counting on you. You're on in five minutes."

The general manager rode off, shouting orders to a group of cowboys who were trying to guide a longhorn steer into a pen.

Will blushed and shook his head. He looked at the cowboys and at the steer. That was the same steer that Bill Pickett was going to jump on and wrestle, right out there in front of that huge crowd.

Those cowboys, even with the general manager yelling orders at them, weren't having much luck. The steer was getting angrier by the second.

Well, he supposed he would have to be brave tonight, but *just* tonight, by golly. He'd quit first thing in the morning. He'd take a train back home and settle down once and for all. Will guessed he could handle that steer all right. But all those people staring at him—that was what scared him most.

The cowboys finally worked the steer into the pen that led to the arena, but the steer was really angry now. Its eyes rolled. Its gray horns, four feet long and sharp as spears, scraped against

246

the boards of the pen.

Bill Pickett led his pony over to the pen and leaned against a post while he studied the steer's movements—the way it twisted its head, the way it hunched its shoulders and bucked.

Will rode over to study the steer, too. His job as "hazer" was to race on the far side of that steer when it came slam-banging out of the pen into the arena. That way, the steer would charge in a fairly straight line so that Bill Pickett could make a clean jump onto its back, grip his strong hands around its horns, and start wrestling it to the ground. If Pickett missed the jump, Will would have to lasso the raging steer and give Pickett a chance to scramble back onto his pony. If Pickett made his jump safely—and he usually did —Will's job would then be to race around the steer, grab Pickett's pony, and lead it away from the struggle.

Bill Pickett looked worried. Like most brave and strong men, he loved animals. He was the only cowboy in the West who could perform the mighty feat of a flying leap onto a fifteen-hundred-pound steer, and then wrestle with it for two, three, and sometimes five minutes around the arena. Pickett considered it a test of skill, like any other wrestling match, but he never wanted to injure a steer. Besides, a steer as angry as this one could mean real trouble!

"Look at that steer jump," Pickett muttered to himself. "I sure hope that arena fence is high enough."

It was time to go on now. Will's heart began to pound as he and Pickett followed the general manager out into the arena. Will looked up at the crowd. It was like being at the bottom of a canyon, he thought, but the canyon walls, instead of being rock, were made up of thousands of men, women, and children. They were all quiet now, all staring down at the three of them. Bill Pickett's act had been advertised as the most "stupendous, death-defying event" in the show. In a daze, Will lifted his hand and waved to that canyon of faces, just as Bill Pickett did. Then, while the general manager introduced them, Will edged his pony back to the left-hand side of the gate where the steer was penned. Bill Pickett cantered his pony over to the right-hand side and sat there waiting.

The general manager rode back beneath the grandstand, and gave a signal.

Some cowboys began beating the sides of the pen with sticks and shouting, "Hi ya! Git, git, git!"

The gate was flung open. The steer raced through it at a dead run, its head waving, its horns gleaming like huge, curved spears. Will spurred his pony in close to the steer. The steer ducked away. Pickett was there on the other side, poised for his jump.

Then, quick as lightning, the steer changed its course again. It darted in front of Pickett's pony and raced toward the high board fence that separated the arena from the crowd! Its head went up. Its legs tensed. In a flash it hurtled over the fence, landed on all fours, bellowed, and clattered up the steps between two rows of people!

"Up!" Bill Pickett yelled to his pony. The pony leaped, cleared the fence, and raced up the steps behind the steer.

The crowd roared. Will didn't hear them. He felt a numbness deep down inside as he spurred his pony and leaped over the fence, too. Somehow he had failed. Now with an enraged steer pounding up that canyon of faces, dozens of people might be trampled or gored.

There was one chance. Will reached down for his lasso and began twirling it as his pony raced behind Pickett's. If the steer kept on the steps and didn't get among the people, it might be possible to rope it at the next landing.

The steer held straight between the lines of screaming people, took the first landing in one leap, and sprinted up the second row of steps. Bill Pickett leaned forward, urging his pony to greater speed.

Will's rope sang in a tight circle around his head. He had been practicing rope tricks ever since he could walk. But this was the smallest space he'd ever worked in, riding up a narrow flight of stairs with people yelling and tumbling over one another all the way up.

The steer reached the second landing and hesitated. Its head swerved for a jump straight into the crowd. As Bill Pickett's pony touched the landing, Pickett leaped at the steer. He landed square on the steer's back, his hands desperately grasping for the horns. If he could reach them, just one twist would veer the creature from its deadly plunge into the crowd! Pickett's huge muscles bulged in the effort as the steer tensed for the jump.

Then Will's lasso snapped over the horns, jerked tight, and yanked the head back!

Up shot Pickett's steely hands. He grabbed the horns and twisted and threw every ounce of weight and strength he had against the steer's neck and forelegs.

The steer crashed to the floor.

Pickett held on, his face twisted in pain, while Will quickly tied two loops around the steer's kicking hind legs and yanked. The hoofs clicked together. The steer bawled and then lay still.

The screams and shouts of the crowd turned into a cheer. The steer started to struggle again. But Bill Pickett leaned over and began humming a range song, just as a mother soothes a frightened baby.

Soon the steer was calm enough so they could lead it away. Will was suddenly aware of all those people again, and was blushing beet red.

The next day, Will walked into the general manager's office. The general manager had the morning papers spread out on his desk. His eyes were beaming.

"I guess you know I was about to quit last night," Will said.

The general manager kept on beaming.

"Well," Will gulped and went on. "After the way I bobbled things, I guess I'd better be getting my bags packed." He hung his head. His hands tugged against his belt for a second, then slid into his pockets.

"You might have a look at the papers before you start packing," the general manager said.

Will looked up. The general manager leaned back in his chair and started laughing. He pointed toward the newspapers.

Will saw his own picture staring at him from the front pages of the papers. COWBOY ROPER A HERO . . . LASSOS MAD STEER LOOSE IN GARDEN'S CROWDS . . . WILL ROGERS AND BILL PICKETT SAVE SCORES FROM LUNGING BEAST. His name was in every newspaper on the desk!

Will began blushing.

"Quit?" the general manager sputtered. "You can't quit! Why, you're ready to have a roping act of your own."

Will Rogers

Will's full name was William Penn Adair Rogers. The world came to know him as Will Rogers, "The Cowboy Philosopher." He became one of the greatest humorists in America. He is still regarded as one of the best ropers of all time. His blushing and his gentle wit made people around the world love him. The mad race up the steps of Madison Square Garden in New York City that night more than fifty years ago began Will's career.

Will Rogers continued to be one of the most popular men in the United States until his death in an airplane crash in Alaska.

Statues of Will Rogers stand in Washington, D. C., and in his home town, Claremore, Oklahoma.

More To Read

Will Rogers, Boy Roper by Donald and Beth Day. Published by Houghton Mifflin Co., Boston, 1950.

THE GREATEST BASEBALL PLAYER IN THE WORLD

Morning came to Johnny's hospital room with a sunbeam and a white-uniformed nurse. The sunbeam danced mischievously through the half-open curtains. And the nurse bustled around Johnny's hospital bed. First she swished open the curtains. A flood of light brightened the room. She filled a little pitcher by Johnny's bed with cold water. She patted, poked, and tucked Johnny's bed into order. Then she said, "Is there anything I can get for you?"

Johnny's eyes flickered open, and he answered weakly, "My scrapbook, please."

When the nurse handed Johnny the battered, bulging scrapbook, the boy's whole face changed. His eyes opened up wide.

His thin little hands eagerly opened the scrapbook.

By Jeannie Peterson

There, on the first page, was a big picture of Johnny's hero—Babe Ruth. Babe looked big and powerful in the picture. He was swinging a baseball bat, and there was a grin on his face. It seemed to Johnny that Babe Ruth was grinning right out of the picture at him.

"He's the greatest baseball player in the world," Johnny said to the nurse. "Whenever Babe's at bat, a pitcher doesn't have a chance. Babe can bat a fast ball right out of any baseball park."

The nurse smiled as Johnny showed her the rest of his scrapbook. It was filled with stories about Babe Ruth hitting home runs and winning ball games. There were other pictures in the scrapbook, too, pictures of Babe Ruth batting, pitching, sliding into home plate, catching fly balls out in right field, and waving to his fans.

After the nurse left, Johnny continued to leaf through the book. But soon he grew tired and dozed off into the dream world of baseball and Babe Ruth.

When Johnny woke up, he could hear voices that came from the corridor outside his room. He recognized the voices of the doctor and his parents.

The doctor was saying, "The boy doesn't seem to want to get well. We've done everything possible for him, but he is getting weaker every day. We don't know how much longer he will last."

Johnny's father said, "He hardly even looks up when his mother and I walk into the room. The only time he seems to have any interest in life is when he's looking at his scrapbook."

Then another man's voice spoke up. It didn't belong to the doctor, or to Johnny's father. The voice said, "Well, I'm glad you called to tell me about Johnny. We'll see what we can do to cheer the little fellow up."

And the tall stranger that belonged to the voice strode into Johnny's room.

"Hiya, keed," the stranger said.

He was just about the biggest man Johnny had ever seen—a giant of a man with broad shoulders and a broad grin. He wore a camel's-hair coat, and a flat camel's-hair cap.

Johnny shook his head and blinked his eyes. I must still be dreaming, he thought.

"How're you doing, Johnny?" the man asked.

Suddenly, Johnny felt so happy that he could hardly speak. The man standing at the foot of his bed was his hero, Babe Ruth!

"Gee, is that really you, Babe?" he finally managed to say.

"Yep, and look what I have for you," Babe Ruth laughed. He held out the shiniest, most beautiful baseball bat that Johnny had ever seen. "This is for you, Johnny, and I expect you'll be able to use it pretty soon."

Johnny was so weak, he could hardly hold the bat, but he managed to take it with both hands.

"This is the most wonderful bat I've ever seen," Johnny said. "Is this the kind of bat you use when you hit your home runs?"

"Well, the bats I use would be pretty heavy for a boy your age," the Babe answered as he took his cap off. "But this one is just as good. You'll be able to give a ball a good swat with it."

Johnny's face glowed with excitement. He still couldn't believe that the great Babe Ruth was in his hospital room. Johnny's words came out so fast that they stumbled over each other.

"Babe, will you tell me what it's really like playing baseball for the Yankees, and hitting home runs all the time, and—?"

Babe held up his hand. "Slow down, Johnny, you'll get winded that way. Just sit back and relax, and I'll tell you all about it."

So the most famous baseball player in the world sat down beside Johnny and started telling him about baseball.

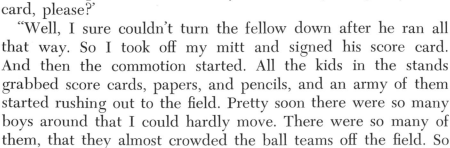

Babe told him about each of the New York Yankee ball players, about the noise and excitement of a World Series game, and about the fans that packed the stadium.

"Do many kids my age go to see you play?" Johnny asked.

"They sure do, son," replied Babe. He settled his broad shoulders back against the chair. "Why one afternoon I was playing out in right field when all of a sudden a little guy about your size came dashing out onto the field. He ran up to me, held out a score card, and a pencil, and said, 'Hey, Babe, will you sign my score card, please?'

"Well, I sure couldn't turn the fellow down after he ran all that way. So I took off my mitt and signed his score card. And then the commotion started. All the kids in the stands grabbed score cards, papers, and pencils, and an army of them started rushing out to the field. Pretty soon there were so many boys around that I could hardly move. There were so many of them, that they almost crowded the ball teams off the field. So we had to stop the game right there. Nope, I've never been able to refuse a kid something that would make him happy," Babe said.

"Gee," Johnny said. "Would you sign your autograph for me, too?"

"Sure enough, Johnny," Babe said. He reached in his coat pocket and pulled out a brand-new baseball. Then he took a pen and scrawled across the white baseball, "Good Luck, Johnny. Babe Ruth"

"Now, there's something else I want to talk to you about," Babe said seriously.

Johnny listened eagerly.

"Johnny, I want you to do everything the doctor tells you to do. He's trying to make you well again. But he can't do it all alone. You have to help him by wanting to get well, and by trying your best to get well."

"I promise I will," nodded Johnny.

"And if you take care of yourself, you'll soon be out with the other boys, playing with this ball and bat."

"Sure, Babe, I'll try to get better," Johnny promised. Right then, he wanted more than anything else to grow to be a big, powerful ball player like Babe Ruth.

"Well, I have a ball game to play this afternoon," the Babe said. "So I have to be leaving now —is there anything that I can do for you, Johnny?"

Johnny thought for a short moment, then he said, "The thing I'd like best in the whole world is for you to hit a home run in the game this afternoon."

Babe laughed, "Okay, Johnny—I'll do that. I'll hit a homer just for you this afternoon." Then the big fellow put his cap back on. "Good-by, now, Johnny."

"Good-by, Babe—I'll always remember everything you said today."

"And I'll hit that homer for you," the Babe promised as he

waved and walked out of the room.

That afternoon the fans at Yankee stadium cheered wildly when the mighty Babe Ruth hit a home run. But none of them knew what a little boy on a hospital bed knew. And none of them was happier than that little boy, because Johnny knew that Babe Ruth hit that homer just for him.

Twenty years later it was Babe Ruth who was sick. He had just come back from the hospital, when he had a visitor. It was a healthy-looking man about thirty years old. It was Johnny!

"Mr. Ruth, I've come back to thank you," Johnny said. "Twenty years ago you gave me a baseball bat and a baseball. But you gave me much more than that. You gave me a will to recover—and that saved my life. Thank you, Babe."

Babe Ruth just smiled modestly and said, "I knew you'd make it, Johnny."

Babe Ruth, baseball's most famous player, was a big man with a big heart. And he was big on the baseball field, too.

The Babe broke most existing baseball records, and then he broke the records that he himself had made. During the years he was playing, he had more home runs, more runs batted in, and more long hits than any other player. In fact, he did more of almost anything a baseball player can do. During his lifetime, he captured or shared sixty-one baseball records. And most of them have never been broken.

But Babe Ruth captured more than records—he captured the hearts and imaginations of millions of American boys like Johnny.

More To Read

Babe Ruth; The Big Moments of the Big Fellow by Tom Meany. Published by Grosset & Dunlap, Inc., New York, 1951.

Young Baseball Champions by Steve Gelman. Published by W. W. Norton & Company, Inc., New York, 1966.

One of the most famous home runs in baseball history:
Babe Ruth points to a spot in the bleachers and hits the ball to that spot.

Babe Ruth was among the first to be elected to
the National Baseball Hall of Fame (*above*) in
Cooperstown, New York.

BIRD WOMAN AND FLAMING HAIR

By Clare Thorne

In the white man's books I am called Bird Woman. My real name is Sacagawea (Sak uh guh WEE uh).

When I was a girl, my people, the Shoshoni Indians, came down from the mountains every summer to camp on the buffalo plains. Our fathers hunted, and our mothers dried the meat so there would be food in our lodges the next winter.

One day, in my ninth year, a scout rode into camp to warn us that a war party of a hundred Minataree braves was coming up the riverbank. Our Shoshoni warriors laughed at the foolish enemy. Our braves were more than twice a hundred.

But the war party of Minatarees carried shining sticks that spoke lightning and thunder. I learned later that these sticks are called guns, and that the Minatarees got them from the white man. On that terrible morning, our hunters who were not killed rode back, shouting that the women and children must hide themselves. Everything was confusion. I ran toward the place where my elder brother, Black Bow, had gone to hide.

All at once I came to the bank of the river, and there, just below me, were four Minatarees on horses!

It was too late to hide myself. I tried to cross the river. But before I was halfway across, one of the Minatarees caught me. He seized my arm and pulled me up on his horse in front of him. He was Red Arrow, the Minataree, who took me with him all the way back to his village on the Big River that white men call the Missouri.

Red Arrow was a man of good heart. He and his wife were kind to me. They treated me like a daughter, but I was not happy in their lodge, which was made of mud like a prairie dog's home.

I passed many years in the village on the Big River. Then one night Red Arrow played the betting game with a white trader named Charbonneau. This was a man who did not speak with a straight tongue, and Red Arrow lost everything. Having lost all other things except his lodge, he used me as his bet, and he lost me, too. That is how I, Sacagawea, came to be the wife of Charbonneau, the trader.

Charbonneau was a boaster and of little courage, but he was father to the little son who was born to me. I tried to do all I could for his comfort. But more and more my heart longed for my home in the mountains.

One day there came to the village of Earth Houses some white men. They were sent by their Great White Chief to find the trail west, across the plains, over the high mountains, and to the Everywhere-Salt-Water. They asked the Minatarees for guides who could show them the trail and who could trade with my people, the Shoshoni. My people, the Shoshoni, owned many horses, and the Americans needed horses to cross the mountains.

My man, Charbonneau, offered to be their guide. For once I was glad. I thought, now I will take my little son in my blanket and follow the Big River to its roots in my mountains. Once we are with my people, the Shoshoni, they will buy our freedom, and we will remain with them forever.

There were two white chiefs. The tall one was named Lewis, but the Minatarees called him Long Knife. The young one had hair the color of a woodfire. His name was Clark, but I called him Flaming Hair.

Soon we started up the Big River. We had thirty-three people in two large boats and six small boats. As we approached my mountains, I grew impatient at our slowness. One day I spoke of it.

Long Knife was impatient, too. "Before long, heavy rains will fall in the mountains," he said. "If we do not find your people and buy horses, it will be too late. We will have to turn back."

"And if we do that?" I asked.

"We will not take this trail again."

That night I prayed to my mountain gods not to close the way they had opened to Sacagawea, but to show me the trail to my people, the Shoshoni. Next morning, I saw smoke on the side of the mountain ahead of us.

It was a sign. Shoshoni scouts had seen us. They were calling my people together. They would lie in wait and destroy us. There was no time to lose now.

"We must run up the trail quickly, before the Shoshoni have gathered!" I told Flaming Hair.

"You can't run, Bird Woman. Not with the baby in your blanket," he said to me.

"We can't go now anyway," said Charbonneau. "There's a storm coming. We must wait till it passes."

But I would not listen to either of them. I started up the trail, holding my blanket tight around me so that my little son rode on my back like a hunter on his pony. Flaming Hair and Charbonneau followed. Before we had come to the foot of the mountain, the first drops of rain fell.

Charbonneau shouted that we must turn back and seek shelter. Flaming Hair saw a cave on the side of the dry riverbed, and we all ran to it. There we were safe in a fine dry place, or so we thought at first. But the rain kept falling.

Soon Charbonneau was grumbling louder than ever, "If this keeps up, there will be a flood down the riverbed."

For once he spoke truth. In my mountains there are floods that come like a wall of water. As we listened, we could already hear a deep rumbling sound.

"We must not wait here," I told Flaming Hair. "The water wall may soon reach the mouth of this cave."

"All right, let's run for it! Down the riverbed and up the far side! That's easier!"

I started, but I slipped and fell.

It was Flaming Hair who helped me and my little son all the way down the riverbed and across the stream that had already formed at the bottom. Then he started up the far side, pulling me after him. In our ears was the roar of the water coming. If we fell, it would be to death on the rocks below. If we climbed too slowly, the wall of water would reach up and snatch us.

But Flaming Hair did not stop. Once the young tree he was holding came loose at the roots. I would have let go so as not to drag him down with us, but he held my wrist and found another tree to pull up by. At last, we reached safety on a wide ledge, high above the water.

I could not speak my thanks to Flaming Hair, but in my heart I made a promise I would help him in something as big as what he had done for us.

As we followed the trail up the mountain, I heard the beating of horses' hoofs.

"Stand back and let me be the one to greet whoever is riding down on us," I said.

Flaming Hair and Charbonneau hid themselves in the brush at the side of the trail, and I stood alone, facing the riders.

"My people, my brothers!" I called as soon as I could see them. "Do not shoot your arrows! It is I—Sacagawea—your sister, long lost to you!"

They reined in their horses, and looked down at me.

"Sacagawea?" they said softly. "Yes, it is you."

They took me to my brother, Black Bow. He was now chief of the Shoshoni.

I called to Flaming Hair and Charbonneau. A runner was sent to bring Long Knife and the rest. When they had come, I spoke for both sides.

Long Knife asked if our people knew the trail to the Everywhere-Salt-Water. Black Bow told him the way.

Long Knife asked them if Black Bow would sell horses to the white chiefs. Black Bow said to tell him that our people had few horses to spare, but they would take counsel of the other Shoshoni tribes and give an answer the next day.

That night I sat in the lodge of my brother, and he told me of all that had happened to our people since I, Sacagawea, had been captured.

"We starve, Younger Sister. The plains are dark with buffalo. But we dare not hunt there because the plains tribes kill our people with the white man's shining sticks. We die of hunger here in the mountains. I have sent messages to all the Shoshoni tribes."

"What messages?" I asked him.

"To come and help us kill these white chiefs."

"Brother!" I cried. "They have done you no evil. Why should you kill them?"

"Our people die for lack of the shining sticks. Your chiefs carry them. Either they die or we must."

I was angry, and that gave me courage to speak against my brother. "By killing the white chiefs you will not feed our people. After one fight with the plains tribes, you will have no more of the guns' food. Be wise, O my brother," I begged him. "Be friends with the white chiefs. They are as straight as the straightest pine tree."

"Very well," he said. "We will sell them horses and buy your freedom."

My freedom! How long I had dreamed of it, and of living with my little son in the lodge of my brother! But without me the white chiefs would never find their trail's end. I told this to Black Bow.

"What is that to you, Sacagawea? What if they do not find the Everywhere-Salt-Water?"

"I have made a promise," I told him. "I have promised to help Flaming Hair, who saved me and my little son. When I have done that, I will be free to return to my people."

So it was that I went with the white chiefs all the way to the Everywhere-Salt-Water, to the place where angry waves rush on the shore even when no wind blows.

I fulfilled my secret promise to help Flaming Hair.

Today, in the city of Helena, Montana, there is a statue of Sacagawea, Long Knife, and Flaming Hair. It stands in memory of the help the Indian girl gave to her friends, Meriwether Lewis (Long Knife) and William Clark (Flaming Hair).

It was because of Sacagawea's help that Lewis and Clark were able to blaze a new trail across the West to the Pacific Ocean. Their journey started a new era of trading in the western territories. Their records gave us important information about the ways of the Indian tribes they met along the way.

After Sacagawea had guided Long Knife and Flaming Hair to the Everywhere-Salt-Water, which we call the Pacific Ocean, she returned to her mountains in search of her Shoshoni people. It was many years before she was able to find them again. By that time, her little son had grown to manhood. Clark had seen to it that Sacagawea's son was educated in the white man's schools. It was Clark's way of showing his thanks for the help Sacagawea had given to him and to his friends.

The Pacific Ocean at the mouth
of the Columbia River on the▶
Washington-Oregon border

More To Read

Winged Moccasins; The Story of Sacajawea by Frances J. Farnsworth. Published by Julian Messner, New York, 1954.

Trails West and Men Who Made Them by Edith Dorian and W. N. Wilson. Published by McGraw-Hill Book Company, New York, 1955.

"GIVE

ME

STRENGTH!"

By Bonnie MacConnell

Two policemen stood outside a big hospital. It was almost dawn. Their hours of work were nearing an end.

"It's been a cool night even for April and it's been quieter than usual," Officer Parquet said. He removed his helmet and ran his fingers through his thick hair. "Now it looks as if it will be a fine day."

Officer Fenner agreed, "Yes, it has been quiet—almost too quiet. Don't you sometimes have a feeling that when it's too quiet something is about to happen?"

Officer Parquet pulled a large handkerchief from his hip pocket. He wiped his forehead and polished the badge on the front of his helmet. "I've often had that feeling," he said.

The words were scarcely spoken when there was a shock, a jolt like a great explosion, a sound like strong winds rushing, a roar like great ocean waves breaking on rocks. The earth shuddered beneath them and hurled both men off their feet. Officer Parquet was thrown against the base of the hospital doorway. His friend, Max Fenner, was thrown to the sidewalk.

A grinding, creaking, rasping sound rose above the earth's terrible rumbling. Officer Parquet saw a chunk of concrete as big as a buggy come crashing down on his companion. The crash was so violent and so sudden that Officer Parquet knew his fellow officer had felt nothing. His friend was dead!

Suddenly, Parquet heard shrieks of terror and agony from within the hospital. The roof had collapsed and whole sections of brick walls lay in heaps of rubble. The fallen roof would soon smother the people trapped inside if it had not already crushed them.

The policeman saw his own helmet smashed by a bounding

piece of concrete. He knew that only a few feet away patients, doctors, and nurses were trapped in the ruins of the hospital.

Officer Parquet turned his head, staring in horror at the destruction that lay in every direction. Then he noticed the wooden pavilion directly across the street. Not a board seemed out of place in the big barnlike building. Suddenly, he realized why the old wooden building still stood. "Thank God!" he said aloud. "My home is made of wood, too! The pavilion has stood the shock because wood gives a little without breaking. My home will be safe!"

The knowledge that his home must have withstood the shock and that his family was probably safe gave him courage to face the job that lay before him.

Screams of injured people and animals came from all around him. Many of the horses that pulled wagons filled with fruits and vegetables to the hospital had been struck by falling bricks. They whinnied and screamed with pain and terror while people, unable to rescue them, stood helplessly by.

As Officer Parquet started to rise another shock came—and another. He fell to the sidewalk again.

He lost track of time. Each moment seemed endless. He saw the pavement rise and twist and buckle like the boiling of thick pudding. He saw wide cracks appear in the ground and he could see distant buildings crumble as if they were sinking into the earth. At last he managed to scramble to his feet.

He staggered blindly in the dust from falling brick, mortar, and plaster to make his way into the ruins of the hospital.

Alone in the silvery dawn, he tore away whole chunks of fallen roof and ceiling. Barehanded, he moved great sections of stone and

fallen bricks, and crept, an inch at a time, into the buried hospital.

He did not notice his own bleeding fingers while he pulled away rubble to reach the people trapped inside.

The head doctor of the hospital lay pinned by debris near a fallen wall. Officer Parquet dragged him free. He saw two patients nearby underneath the wall. "Doctor, if you're able to walk, go outside," he said.

"First I must reach those patients," the doctor replied.

"Go outside," Officer Parquet repeated. "You are needed there. I will bring the patients to the pavilion across the street. It is still standing and looks secure. There are many injured people who need help. I will work here. You are needed there."

By now fires had started. They burned in every direction! The whole city seemed ablaze and the flames seemed to be creeping closer. The air was foul with heavy smoke. Officer Parquet's eyes burned and watered as he staggered, again and again, across the broken and twisted street, from the ruined hospital to the pavilion.

"How many more people are trapped there? God, give me strength to carry them all," he prayed.

Officer Parquet had dug an area like a small tunnel from the hospital to the street. As he worked his way through it, carrying the injured across his strong shoulders, bricks and broken concrete blocks continued to fall.

We might be hit at any moment, he thought.

On each trip through the narrow opening he tried to speak a word of encouragement if the person on his back was conscious. His strength was failing fast and each time it became more of an effort to speak. He was blind with dizziness but he followed a now familiar trail.

He tried laying the injured on a mattress to drag them to safety, but the rubble was far too high. He had to carry them.

He stopped for a moment, shaking his head to clear his vision when he saw a man staggering about inside the hospital. "Here, let me help you. How did you get in here?" He seized the man's arm to lead him out.

"I came to the hospital for help but the hospital's gone. I'm hurt. The building where I live fell in. A bunch of us got caught. Guess I'm lucky though."

"Everyone of us still alive is lucky," Officer Parquet said.

He grabbed the man's arm and guided him toward the pavilion. The man's legs collapsed under him, almost pulling the policeman down with him. But Officer Parquet kept his balance and helped the injured man to stand again. He guided the man into the pavilion.

Then once more he turned his steps wearily toward the hospital. Halfway across he saw an uninjured man hurrying along, climbing over piles of rubble.

Parquet's voice was hoarse when he called,

"Mister, can you give me a little help?"

But the man did not even look around.

An aching knot formed in the policeman's throat. All his tiredness seemed to strike him at once. As he reached the spot where the hospital door had stood, his legs started to buckle under him. He looked after the man hurrying away and he dropped down to rest on a large piece of concrete. I've done enough. I can't go on, he said to himself.

More people were walking about now. Most of them were carrying things which they thought were valuable. A man and a woman struggled with a heavy grandfather's clock. A small boy right behind them clutched a battered toy steam engine to his bare chest.

If I could only have a little of the strength these people are wasting on foolish things! Officer Parquet said to himself. But sheer weariness overcame him. He dropped his head into his hands. Why should I, who have worked all night long, have to do so much while so many others do nothing? he wondered.

He saw his bloody hands for the first time. Then he noticed his torn clothing and his crushed helmet, which lay a few feet away. And there, not more than a foot from where he sat, Max Fenner's body had been crushed by falling concrete from the wall of the hospital.

Suddenly, he heard another faint cry, hardly more than a whisper of pain from the hospital. Officer Parquet raised his head.

He forgot his aching, bleeding hands, his weary legs, and all the terror-shocked people who seemed to be doing nothing to help.

Tremblingly, he rose to his feet, and went in to carry the very last patient from the ruins of the hospital to the safety of the pavilion.

Edward F. Parquet, the policeman in this story, became a hero that day. He saved all the patients, nurses, and doctors in San Francisco's Central Emergency Hospital.

The terrible disaster that struck San Francisco that day was an earthquake. A good part of the city was destroyed by the earthquake and by the fires that resulted from it. Hundreds of people were killed and thousands of buildings were destroyed.

San Francisco, just after the earthquake

But the brave people of San Francisco rebuilt their city to the bigger, better, safer city it is today.

The San Francisco Earthquake struck in 1906. Many of the people who were there are still alive today. And it is possible that some of them can thank Officer Edward F. Parquet for saving their lives.

More To Read

All About Volcanoes and Earthquakes by Frederick H. Pough. Published by Random House, New York, 1953.

Key to San Francisco by Charlotte Jackson. Published by J. B. Lippincott Company, Philadelphia, 1961.

the SECRET of the CAVE

BY HELEN KAYE MILLER

The horse-drawn cart bumped and jogged through the yellowing fields in Spain. The cart wheels whined for grease, and the horse's hoofs made an up-and-down squish and plop in the thick mud. From deep within the collar of her overcoat, Maria giggled and chanted, with a five-year-old's delight in sounds, "I'm going to Altamira, Altamira, Altamira."

Don Marcelino de Sautuola, her father, smiled and gently rumpled his daughter's soft, thick hair.

"Is it a big, big cave, Father?"

"Yes, Maria, a very big cave. So big that not even I know the whole of it, and I have been working in it for more than a year."

"Tell me again about those people—you know, the ice people."

Don Marcelino laughed, "Not ice people, my darling, but people who lived when more than half the world was covered with ice. It was so long ago that we can scarcely begin to imagine it. And in the Cave of Altamira I have found some of the tools the people used. Think of that!"

Maria nodded her head, even though she didn't understand. Then she cried, "Our horse is stopping! Why is he stopping, Father?"

"Because he knows we are at the Cave of Altamira." He lifted the tiny child from the cart. Maria stood for a moment, not knowing what to do next. The spiky meadow grasses tickled her legs. Don Marcelino gathered his digging tools under one arm and a blanket and food basket under the other.

With a wink, he said, "Wait here for just a moment, Maria."

Then he strode off. He seemed to vanish completely—like the magicians in the tales he told to Maria at bedtime.

Maria's heart began thumping with fright at being left alone. But nearly at once Don Marcelino's tall, broad form reappeared. He came back to pick up some oil lamps and to scoop Maria onto his shoulder.

"Now you are going to see something surprising and marvelous, Maria," he said. "We are going down into the ground and into a big cave. It will be cool and dark down there, but you won't be afraid with me there, will you?"

"No, Father," replied Maria earnestly. "Not with you." She brushed his cheek lightly with a butterfly kiss, then watched in wonder and excitement as the flat surface of the meadow gave way to a sudden slope that carried them down sharply into a narrowing passage. Ahead of them she could see a black opening. Even before they reached it, the sweet odor of the meadow changed to musty dampness—a little like that of their fruit and wine cellar at home. But here there was no fragrance of ripening fruit and aging wine—only the damp and chill of underground.

So little light followed them from outdoors that Maria could see nothing at all at first. But before long she began to make out some dim outlines of curving walls and a rounded ceiling. She stayed very still after Don Marcelino lifted her from his shoulder, waiting for him to light the lanterns. And it was hard to stand still and straight because the floor was so slanty.

This is what it would be like to stand on the roof of the servants' cottage, she thought. But the air—I don't like it. It's like rain without wetness. It is so heavy I can push it, and the smell hurts my nose.

In the soft glow of the lanterns she saw her father smiling down at her. That made her feel better, so she smiled, too. Now suddenly brave and happy, she ran a short distance up the slanted dirt floor, then whirled to look all around her as far as the light from the flickering lanterns would allow. How big, oh, how big this cave room was. It stretched far out on all sides. As she looked and looked as far as her eyes could see, a strange feeling came over her. She stopped her whirling and dancing and became very still and very solemn. The cave seemed so vast and silent. She felt all tingly and shivery, but not exactly afraid.

"You can help dig, Maria," said Don Marcelino. He gave her a short-handled spade. She was happy and gay again and dug excitedly in a spot near her father. She watched his actions closely and imitated them. When he would kneel, she would kneel. When he sifted the loose dirt through his fingers, she did too. And it was in comical tones very like his that she would pick up an object and mutter, "Not an Ice Age knife, only a stone," and would throw the object away.

But soon Maria was tired of digging. She wanted to run and play. Several times she ran up the slanting floor and down again. That was fun. Then she noticed how bumpy the ceiling was. She stood on tiptoe, leaned her head far back and squinted her eyes for a really good look. Lamplight is hard to see by, so she wasn't sure at first.

Then she was sure.

"Up there, Father! Please look!"

"The bumps, Maria? They're like warts on a frog. I've seen them." He kept on digging.

"But see the pictures, Father! Cows, I think. And they're running and jumping and lying down. The pictures are all over, everywhere!"

"Such an imagination," said Don Marcelino with

a hearty laugh that echoed through the cave. "They couldn't be pictures. No one has ever heard of artists in the Ice Age. They're shadows, maybe. The flicker of the light is playing tricks on you."

As he bent down to examine a clod of newly turned earth, Maria crouched beside him and tugged at his sleeve.

"Please, Father, I want you to see them, too."

Don Marcelino looked at her small face turned so earnestly and intently to his own.

"All right, then. But you must promise not to be disappointed."

He rose, grasped a lantern, and swung it high. As its radiance spread over the lumpy outline of the stone ceiling, he gasped and almost let the lantern drop.

"Maria, oh, Maria," he murmured in a tone so weak and faltering that she ran to him and clutched his leg, ready to help with her slight strength in case he fell. His hand came to rest lightly and briefly on her head, then he straightened and she let go. Holding the lamp high, he began to walk—now fast, now slow. She followed, her head tilted far backward like his until her neck ached with the strain, and she watched and listened.

"See, they *are* pictures," Maria said.

"How could I have missed them in all these months," her father murmured. "And we're the first! Not in ten thousand years —*at least* ten thousand years—could there have been any other eyes to look on this!"

He kept talking in a rapid, whispering way as his light flashed overhead.

"How vivid, how lifelike! Here's a great, strong bison struck by a spear and huddled and crumpled over. Its coat is so glossy that it could be alive! And isn't this amazing? The artist used these natural bumps of the ceiling as part of the painting. It's not just painting and not just sculpture, but a little of both!"

Don Marcelino stood and looked and marveled at the pictures on the ceiling for a long time.

At last, they prepared to leave. But when they reached the mouth of the cave, Don Marcelino turned for one last look before leaving the chill and the dark. As the warm sunlight fell on them once again, Maria felt his lips graze her hair and heard his voice sounding deep and muffled, "Thank you, thank you, my dear little girl!"

The discovery of the paintings on the ceiling of the Altamira Cave was one of the most important discoveries ever made in the study of prehistory.

Maria de Sautuola became a famous woman. She met kings and noblemen during her lifetime. Noted scientists called her discovery one of the wonders of the world, a precious work of art, one of man's finest creations.

But for Maria nothing ever matched the thrill she knew on that long-ago afternoon in 1879 when she and her father were the first persons in more than ten thousand years to look at the Altamira paintings, and when Don Marcelino's voice, husky with emotion, said, "Thank you, oh, thank you, my dear little girl!"

If you are ever at the northern edge of Spain that lies along the Bay of Biscay, you can visit the Caves of Altamira and see the paintings that Maria saw on the ceiling.

One of the Altamira cave paintings

More To Read

The First Men in the World by Anne Terry White. Published by Random House, New York, 1953.

The Story of Caves by Dorothy Sterling. Published by Doubleday & Company, Inc., New York, 1956.

Deep Down: Great Achievements in Cave Exploration by Garry Hogg. Published by Criterion Books, Inc., New York, 1962.

"WE'RE GOING OUT
BIRD SHOOTING!"

By Jeannie Peterson

Spring burst out of hiding, and suddenly the world was awake again. Earth's long, cold winter was over. The birds twittered and sang high in the treetops, and the sun broke from behind winter's clouds, brightening the air.

The day was awake, but the little country village was still asleep. The sun shone over shuttered houses and quiet cobblestone streets.

Then the sound of running footsteps broke the morning silence. They grew louder, and louder. And a boy came running down the street.

Henry was puffing from his early morning run. He stopped in front of one of the houses, and yelled up to an open window, "Hey, Albert! Wake up!"

No answer.

"A A L L L L L L L L L B E R R T!" Henry's voice echoed throughout the village.

Soon a tousled head appeared at the window. Albert rubbed the sleep from his eyes, and squinted out at the bright sun.

"It's early, Henry—what do you want?" he called to his friend.

"Get your slingshot, Albert. We're going out bird shooting! Hurry and get dressed."

Albert frowned. He didn't really want to go bird shooting.

But Henry yelled up, "Aw, come on slowpoke. Hurry up! Don't be a spoil-sport."

Albert dressed hurriedly, and snatched up his slingshot. And soon the boys were headed for the hills that surrounded the village.

The brown fields had just lost their blanket of snow, and the earth was soft and squishy.

But Henry said, "Down on your knees, Albert. We have to be quiet, so we don't scare the birds away."

The two boys crept over the wet ground. They were headed for a tree that had a whole flock of birds fluttering in its branches.

But Albert hung back. He wasn't at all anxious to shoot a bird. Why did I let Henry drag me out here, anyway? he thought. I guess it's because he'd call me a chicken and a coward if I didn't come. And now, if I don't shoot a bird, Henry will tell the other village boys, and they'll never stop teasing me.

The two boys had reached the tree now, and they crouched under its branches. Albert looked up and saw birds with red-tipped wings flying from limb to limb. How beautiful they looked! How happy they sounded!

Albert shivered when he thought that a stone from his slingshot could change one of those happy creatures into a dead pile of ruffled feathers.

Suddenly, Henry nudged Albert, and whispered, "OK, get your slingshot ready—you get the big bird on that low branch." He was pointing at a beautiful bird that was swinging happily on the branch.

Slowly, Albert drew a stone from his leather pouch. It was a small, smooth stone, and he fingered it gently and examined it, stalling for time.

"Hurry!" Henry whispered.

Reluctantly, Albert put the stone in his sling. He thought, I don't want to do this—I don't want to do it, but I must—

With trembling hands, Albert aimed the slingshot at the beautiful bird with red-tipped wings. He was just about to let the stone fly, when suddenly the bells of the village church rang through the morning air, joining their melodious song with that of the birds. To Albert, they seemed like a message straight from heaven.

With each chime, they seemed to say, "Thou shalt not kill. Thou shalt not kill. Thou shalt not kill." And with each chime, the message was clearer to Albert.

As he listened, he still held his slingshot poised to shoot. Then suddenly he jumped up, gave a loud shout, and shooed the birds away to safety.

Henry looked up angrily, but Albert didn't even notice him.

As he watched the birds flying away, Albert felt warm and good inside. He knew he had done the right thing. A smile crept over his face as he turned back toward the village.

The chime of the bells stayed in his heart. And Albert remembered the message of the bells, "Thou shalt not kill," all his life.

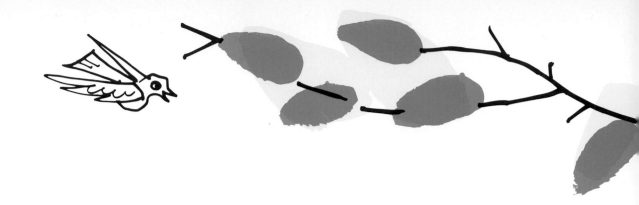

Albert in this story was Albert Schweitzer, a man who did many wonderful things. He became famous as a physician, a writer, a musician, a philosopher, a clergyman, and a missionary. This story took place in a small region on the French-German border, called Alsace.

The words, "Thou shalt not kill," were very important to Albert Schweitzer. When he grew up and became a doctor, he went to a region in Africa which is now called Gabon. He used money he raised to build a hospital. And he devoted his time and skill to caring for the sick and needy. When he won the Nobel peace prize in 1952, he used his award money to expand his hospital, and to comfort those who suffered from disease.

Albert's love for the beautiful bird he couldn't kill as a boy was the same love that he felt for all living things. This is one of the reasons why some people have called Albert Schweitzer "The greatest human being of his time."

More To Read

The Story of Albert Schweitzer by Jo Manton. Published by Abelard-Schuman, Ltd., New York, 1955.

The Story of Albert Schweitzer by Anita Daniel. Published by Random House, New York, 1957.

COULD THEY

By Armstrong Sperry

MAKE IT ?

"It won't be long now, men. Soon we will reach our goal, the South Pole!" the English captain shouted.

A cheer went up from the small band of men. All their months of effort, all the dangers they had faced had been worth it. They were about to become the first human beings to reach the South Pole.

Or were they?

Just then Bowers, one of the explorers, pointed toward something on the surface of the ice.

"Captain! Look!" Bowers cried. "There's something there. It looks like a flag!"

The men struggled toward the object. It was a black signal flag beside the remains of a supply tent.

"We've lost," moaned the captain. "The Norwegians have been here already. Amundsen has won the race for the South Pole."

Sadness gripped the hearts of all the men. They had come this far only to lose the race. There was nothing for them to do now but walk the last few weary miles to the South Pole, and then start the long trip back.

Two days later they arrived at another tent pitched at the Pole. And on top of this tent was a Norwegian flag.

The captain stepped inside the tent. He found two slips of paper. One was a sealed envelope with the inscription: FOR HIS MAJESTY, KING HAAKON VII.

Attached to the envelope was a message addressed to the captain. It read:

> Dear Captain ——
>
> As you are probably the first to reach here after me, I ask you kindly to forward the enclosed letter to King Haakon. If you can use any of the articles I have left, please do so. I wish you safe return.
>
> Yours truly,
> Roald Amundsen

293

Amundsen had reached the South Pole one month ahead of the English explorers. Knowing the dangers of the return journey, Amundsen had left these letters for the captain. If either party made it back, the world would know of Amundsen's success.

The English captain had arrived at the South Pole one month too late. He and his men now had to face the dangers of the return trip after losing the race. And it was almost winter.

They had to retrace their steps eight hundred miles to safety, and the weather would be even worse than it had been. They had to face again barriers of ice, deep crevasses sometimes hidden by snow, and blinding blizzards. Besides himself, each man had to haul nearly two hundred pounds of supplies on a sledge.

The men were weary, and disappointment added to their weariness. Their bearded faces and heavy clothing became starched stiff with ice. Birdie Bowers stumbled into a crevasse, nearly killing himself. Doctor Bill strained a tendon in his leg and walked in pain. Taff Evans had a frostbitten nose and a bad cut that would not heal on his hand. Titus Oates' feet showed signs of frostbite. One of the captain's feet had turned black.

So they traveled on, slowly, for about four weeks. Birdie and Dr. Bill had snow blindness. But they were not so badly off as Evans, who had lost two fingernails from frostbite, and had become so ill he couldn't do his share of the work. The men worried about him. They knew how much he needed the care of doctors. One morning, Evans walked on a little way from the group. The captain warned him not to go far, and watched him as he went. Sometime before noon, he saw the sick man fall to his knees. When the captain and others reached him, they knew Taff Evans couldn't go on. They put up a tent around him, and stayed, until, a few hours later, he died.

Saddened, the men went on. Before long, they were struck with another misfortune. They reached one of their supply depots and found that fuel stored there had evaporated. The leather washers on the oil cans had shrunk in the cold. Now, the men would have no more hot soup or tea. This was serious. Without hot food, how could their bodies stay warm?

Grimly, each man forced himself to keep moving. If they were to make it, they must reach the next supply camp, fifty-five miles away—and soon. The captain tried to cheer his men, but after so much trouble, he had begun to wonder if they could reach safety. He did not know that the worst was yet to come.

It was nearly four weeks since Taff Evans had died. Now, Titus Oates' nose, fingers, and feet were frostbitten. One night, Titus made a decision. He could barely stand up. He could travel no farther. And even if he could, he couldn't keep up with his companions. He had slowed them down long enough. Without him to delay them, he thought, the others might succeed in getting through to the supply camp. He knew that their chances were very slim. But he himself had reached the end of his journey. Painfully, he struggled to his feet and stumbled toward the tent flap.

The captain sat up in his sleeping bag. He called out sharply, "What are you doing, Oates? What has happened?"

Doctor Bill stirred uneasily. He tried to sit up. "Have you lost your senses, man?" he cried weakly.

Birdie Bowers shouted in a hoarse voice, "Come back, Oates, don't be a fool!"

But Titus Oates only mumbled, "Don't worry about me—"

The tent flap flew open. The stricken man staggered outdoors. His companions were too weak to stop him. They could only call out his name.

Oates' one thought was for the safety of the other men. Somehow he managed to tie the tent flap shut before disappearing into the blizzard. Again his companions called out after him. But only the wind answered.

Titus Oates was never seen again.

Sadly, the men moved ahead. The food supply was growing short. The fuel was nearly used up. Blizzards and temperatures of forty degrees below zero made the going almost impossible. There were only three men left now—the captain, Birdie Bowers, and Doctor Bill.

Each night when they made camp they were a few miles closer to the supply camp than they were the night before—twenty-one miles to the camp one night, fifteen miles to the camp the next night, eleven miles the night after. Eleven miles to safety! If only the food and the fuel would hold out.

Then a severe blizzard struck. Travel was impossible. Day after day the blizzard raged. The temperature was down to fifty degrees below zero. The men could not leave the shelter of their tent until the storm let up. And each of them knew that he must keep moving or freeze to death.

When they had been trapped in the tent for over a week, Birdie Bowers asked his leader, "How much food is left, captain?"

"Enough for only one more day."

"And the fuel?"

"Almost gone."

Bowers and Doctor Bill avoided each other's eyes. The two men had complete confidence in the captain. But they knew now that they were in terrible danger.

"Buck up, men!" the captain said as cheerfully as he could manage. "We may as well get some sleep. If the storm eases up by morning, we'll make a dash for the camp. It's only eleven miles away—one day's journey, maybe two at the most. We'll

reach it, never fear."

"Do you really believe we'll get through?" Doctor Bill questioned hopefully.

Birdie Bowers asked, "Can we make it, captain?"

For a moment, the captain was silent. Every muscle in his body ached. His frozen foot sent pain up through his leg. The supply camp was only eleven miles away.

Quietly, he answered, "At least we can try."

The three men wearily crawled into their sleeping bags. Not so long ago the bags had given warmth and shelter after a long day's journey. Now they were stiff with ice.

"If only we didn't have to breathe," said Bowers. "My breath has frozen inside my sleeping bag."

"Mine, too," said Doctor Bill. "It is so cold that our breath has coated almost everything in the tent with ice."

The captain knew that even if the storm ended by morning, it would be nearly impossible to fight through to the supply camp. They still had the will to survive. But the strength had left their bodies.

The captain reached for the diary in which he made a daily entry. His numb fingers closed around the stub of a pencil. Perhaps, at some later date, this diary would be discovered.

For a moment the captain paused, listening to the howl of the storm. His teeth chattered. His body quivered. The wind whistled a shriller blast. The little tent shook. For thousands of miles, no other living human being existed on the lost white continent— only these three, wasted with hunger, huddling together in a tent.

The captain struggled to sit upright. With the remaining drops of fuel he managed to light the lamp. By its wavering glow he saw Doctor Bill and Birdie Bowers. They were huddled deep in their sleeping bags. How many hardships, how many dangers they had faced and survived together! And now—

He spoke to each man by name, softly.

"Doctor Bill?"

There was no answer.

"Birdie?"

Both men must be sleeping.

With great difficulty the captain scrawled these words in his diary:

> "We are very near the end . . . We have been willing to give our lives to this enterprise, for the honor of our country . . ."

The captain laid his pencil down for a moment. He leafed through the pages of his diary. He remembered all the hardships he and his men had faced together. He remembered his disappointment at having reached the Pole a month too late. He remembered the courage of his men and Titus Oates' great sacrifice. And then he remembered the most cruel blow of all—the blizzard that had trapped them in this tent for eight days when they were only eleven miles from safety.

Eleven miles! Could they make it?

He knew now that they couldn't!

Again the captain's numb fingers clutched the pencil. The record must be complete.

> "We shall stick it out to the end, but we are getting weaker, of course, and the end cannot be far . . . for my own sake, I do not regret this journey, which has shown that Englishmen can endure hardships, help one another, and meet death with as great a fortitude as ever in the past . . . It seems a pity, but I do not think I can write more."

The captain signed his name. His hand faltered. The lamp dimmed. The flame snuffed out.

The captain in this story was Robert Falcon Scott, a famous English explorer and naval officer. Captain Scott reached the South Pole on January 18, 1912. Roald Amundsen had been there first, only a month before Scott. Amundsen returned home safely. But Scott and his party had to face the deadly Antarctic winter. Had Captain Scott been able to leave the Antarctic just a few weeks earlier, he and his men might have made it safely home.

Eight months later, at the beginning of the Antarctic summer, a searching party found the bodies of the English explorers. Scott's diary filled in the details of his tragic journey. Roald Amundsen's letter to King Haakon still lay safely within its pages. But by that time the whole world knew that Amundsen had been the first to reach the South Pole.

Captain Robert Falcon Scott had lost his last race, but he had won immortal fame.

More To Read

The First Book of the Antarctic by J. B. Icenhower. Published by Franklin Watts, Inc., New York, 1956.

All About the Arctic and Antarctic by Armstrong Sperry. Published by Random House, New York, 1957.

Robert Falcon Scott

Roald Amundsen

Photograph taken by Captain Scott and his men upon their arrival at the South Pole. The tent and the Norwegian flag were left by Roald Amundsen.

THE SECRET OF THE TALKING LEAVES

By Marion E. Gridley

A group of Indian boys crowded around a man who sat alone by a small fire.

"There he sits—the dreamer! Sequoyah, the lame one, who makes magic with marks," the boys shouted.

At Sequoyah's side were some strips of bark from a birch tree. He had been muttering to himself in a low tone. Now and again he drew a mark on the smooth side of a piece of bark with a sharp stick he had charred in the fire.

"I do not make magic," Sequoyah said. "You are foolish boys to think so. I am making a talking leaf such as the white man has. On what he calls paper, the white man makes many marks. These marks are his thoughts. He can send his paper many miles, and his thoughts will speak out for him."

The boys shook with laughter.

"Sequoyah not only talks to himself, he boasts, too," the leader of the boys, Young Hawk, shouted. "Remember the story of our Cherokee people about the boy who boasted? He was turned into a rabbit. Look! Rabbit ears already start to grow on Sequoyah's head!"

He pointed to some bits of bark that had become entangled in Sequoyah's hair.

Sequoyah's eyes flashed with anger as he rose to his feet.

Quickly tucking something into the wide sash of colored yarn that he wore around his buckskin shirt, Sequoyah said, "I do not boast. Never have I boasted. I have said only that I can do that which I will do."

Again the boys roared with laughter.

"Yes, the lame one will do what no man can do," Young Hawk cried. "He will take the words of the Cherokee people and turn them into marks. He will put the marks on a piece of bark. Then others will look at the marks and understand what is written. He says these

marks written on bark are talking leaves."

Snatching up a piece of bark, Young Hawk held it to his ear. "Speak to me," he said. "Tell me what Sequoyah has told you to say."

Young Hawk held the bark higher, pushing Sequoyah back against a tree.

"This talking leaf says nothing. It makes no sound. It is as foolish as Sequoyah," he said.

Quickly he tossed the piece of bark into the fire. The other boys, too, kicked the strips of bark into the flames while Sequoyah tried to stop them. In a few minutes, nothing was left of the precious bits of bark but a heap of ashes. Sequoyah's years of patient work had been for nothing.

Young Hawk cried out, "The chiefs of our village of Tuskigi even now talk about Sequoyah and what he does. They say that Sequoyah is a magician. We must put an end to his foolishness so that he will be one of us again."

Just then, a drum beat loudly. It was the call to a council meeting. When the drum sounded the council call, everyone had to go. Something important was about to take place.

Hooting and calling, the boys ran away, leaving Sequoyah to himself. Sequoyah's heart pounded with each beat of the great drum. What was the council about? Did Young Hawk speak the truth? Were the chiefs about to punish him? Would his dream of putting Cherokee thoughts down in writing be ended? Surely the chiefs would be glad when they understood about the talking leaf.

As Sequoyah limped toward the council ring, he saw people of the village leaving their log houses to take their places in a circle around the chiefs. By the time he arrived at the council, the rest of the villagers had already assembled. They muttered angrily as Sequoyah came near the circle.

Now the drum beat for attention, and Sequoyah's name was called. Holding his head high, he walked proudly to the center of the council ring.

I will not let them weaken me, he thought. A tree in the storm is strong. Even the small and gentle creatures of the forest have the strength to live and go about their ways. I am lame and I cannot be a hunter or a warrior. But I can be strong. I must make them listen. I must make them understand.

The chief, Bear Man, spoke. His voice was stern, and his face cold and forbidding.

"Sequoyah, we hear bad things about you. We hear that you talk to yourself. That you give foolish answers. That you make magic spells. And that you will bring evil to the Cherokee people. Are these things true, Sequoyah?"

"These things are not true," Sequoyah answered.

"What is the truth?" Bear Man asked.

A murmur spread around the circle.

Then there fell a silence so still that the sounds of the forest could be plainly heard. Sequoyah heard an acorn falling from a bough. He heard the rustle of leaves from the leap of a squirrel. He heard the ripple of water in the nearby river. They were soft sounds, yet from them Sequoyah took heart.

It is a sign that I, too, will be heard, he thought. Bear Man is a wise and good chief. He is willing to give me my chance to save myself.

Aloud, he said, "I shall speak truly. Since I first saw the talking leaves of the white man, I have known that they were not

magic. They are nothing to fear. I have learned their secret."

"And the marks you make, Sequoyah? Do they speak to you?" Bear Man asked.

Sequoyah nodded his head. "Yes, but not out loud. You cannot hear them—you must see them. I will show you."

Sequoyah pulled a knife from his sash and began to outline something in the hard, packed earth.

Quickly he traced some of the strange figures that the people had seen him draw on bark.

Bear Man looked at them closely. "These foolish marks tell me nothing," he said. "Sequoyah is a fool. The people are right."

"Please," Sequoyah begged. "You will understand if I show you a little more. Sparrow, your son, has sometimes watched me. Let me show him one marking. If he can tell you what it says, you will know that I tell the truth."

For a long moment, Bear Man sat in silence.

Trembling, Sequoyah spoke to the chief, "I will tell you—in your ear alone—what a word will be. If Sparrow does not tell you that word, then you may punish me as a magician and a foolish one. But give me this one chance, my chief."

Bear Man did not answer. The waiting was almost unbearable. Again the strange silence fell upon the council ring. Sequoyah's heart pounded as he silently pleaded. Please, Bear Man, please!

It is not the punishment that Sequoyah dreads. It is not the hurt of the jeers and laughter, even though they are sharper than any arrow. It is the talking leaf that is important. Sequoyah cannot give up the talking leaf for it is his dream of great things for his people.

Then came Bear Man's wonderful words, "Send for my son."

When Sparrow came, Sequoyah spoke quietly to the chief. Again, he drew some strange marks on the ground.

"My son, look well upon these marks," Bear Man told Sparrow. "What do they say?"

Shy and frightened, Sparrow hung his head. Sequoyah strained to help him.

"Sparrow, look, remember! Remember the day when you watched me at work? I told you what this was. What did I say? Think, Sparrow. You must think and remember."

"Silence!" Bear Man ordered. "Do not help Sparrow."

Sequoyah looked away.

"What do they say?" Bear Man asked again.

"I don't know," Sparrow said. "You did tell me, Sequoyah, but I can't remember. You said it was a word, a Cherokee word."

Bear Man pointed for Sparrow to leave the council ring. A great sigh went up from the people. The council was over. Sequoyah would be punished.

Just then, Sparrow's face brightened. He ran back to his father. "The word was 'Cherokee,'" he cried.

Bear Man held up his hand for silence. He looked around at the people.

"Sequoyah has spoken truly. This is the word he told me," Bear Man called out. "Now he will tell us about the talking leaves."

"The secret is here," Sequoyah said. He drew something from his sash. It was the thing he had tucked away when the boys came upon him. It was a little spelling book.

"A white man gave me this," he said. "From this book, the white children learn to make talking leaves. This is the secret. The talking leaf says nothing if you do not know the signs. The signs are called letters. To those who know them, the words are understood through the letters. Each word has a meaning. It is the way the letters are placed that so many things can be said."

He opened the book. "I have taken my signs from here," he explained. "But I have made the meanings Cherokee. The Cherokee people speak with sounds. They have many sounds. I say these many sounds over and over to myself. I want to pick a sign from the white man's book for each sound. Then I will teach the marks to any Cherokee who wants to learn. We will have our own talking leaves, our own alphabet. This good, which the white man has, will be ours."

"And when will this be, Sequoyah?" Bear Man asked.

Sequoyah looked down. "Not for a long time," he said. "Today, all of my marks were burned, and I must begin again. It is not easy to catch the sounds, to match them with a mark, to have a different mark for each sound. It all must be done over."

Bear Man stood up and said, "This is not a crazy man or a magician. This is not a foolish person. Sequoyah has the mind of an eagle. It soars high into the sky. And with his eye he sees far beyond the mountains. Sequoyah will teach our sons. The boys that burned his marks will help Sequoyah. They will do whatever he tells them. Some day Sequoyah will give great things to the Cherokee people. I, Bear Man, believe this to be so."

The council was ended.

The words Bear Man spoke that day came true. Sequoyah did give great things to his Cherokee people. He gave them a system of writing that used the Cherokee language. But before he could get his people to accept his system, Sequoyah had to face many difficulties like the ones he faced in this story. Sequoyah's system was so simple that it could be learned in a short time. Soon, thousands of Cherokee could read and write their own language. Before this, the Cherokee had had no way to read or write. Sequoyah made it possible for the Cherokee to open their own schools and to print their own newspapers.

A statue of Sequoyah stands in Statuary Hall in Washington, D.C. The giant redwood trees were named Sequoia in his honor.

Today, the Cherokee people speak English, and Sequoyah's alphabet is no longer in use. But some Cherokee still understand it.

More To Read

The Cherokee: Indians of the Mountains by Sonia Bleeker. Published by William Morrow & Co., Inc., New York, 1952.

Sequoyah: Leader of the Cherokee by Alice Lee Marriott. Published by Random House, New York, 1956.

Where is the Treasure Map?

By Marion West Stoer

Lloyd kicked the footstool. "Still raining! We have had rain for nine days in a row," he complained.

Louis smiled at his stepson. "We'll be in Switzerland soon. The weather should be better there."

Lloyd was sorry he had complained. After all, the main reason he was here was to keep his mother and stepfather company until they would leave Scotland for a climate that would be better for the health of his stepfather, Louis. Lloyd looked at Louis, a tall, lean man hunched over his drawing pad.

Lloyd went to the drawing pad and watched over his stepfather's shoulder as a sketch took shape.

"What do you make of it, Lloyd?" Louis asked excitedly.

"It looks like a fat dragon standing up. But I guess it's really an island."

"Right," Louis said. "There are pirates on this island. Can you see them?"

"Pirates?" Lloyd asked. "What are they doing?"

David Stone Martin

"Hmmmm. Let's see." Louis sketched in some trees and a swamp here and there. "They could be hiding some treasure."

Louis kept sketching while Lloyd's mind raced ahead, bringing him visions of scowling faces peering out from tangled vines and ragged figures creeping quietly through the underbrush with pistols cocked and daggers bared.

"The pirates will have to draw a map to show where they hid their treasure," said Louis. "This is *their* map." His pencil was working quickly now. "Mizzenmast Hill! That's a good name for a landmark."

He drew two smaller islands in a bay at the southern end of the large island.

"What are all those numbers you're putting around the outside of the island?" asked Lloyd. "A code?"

"No, water depth. A pirate map would have to show how deep the water is, so a ship won't go aground. We'll have to show where the tides are strongest, too. When these pirates come back to get their treasure, or to bury more, the one who has this map can guide them in."

"I'd come in by that small island," Lloyd decided. "There seems to be a good water depth behind it. What shall we call it?"

"The small island?" Louis thought for a moment. "How about Skeleton Island?"

"Say, that's good," agreed Lloyd. He pulled up a chair and eagerly scanned the map. He was beginning to feel like one of the pirates himself.

"But it's too small to hide anything on," Louis said. "That's why we have to row across to the larger island."

Lloyd pointed to the spot on the map called Mizzenmast Hill. "Let's head for shore at the foot of that hill. It's too swampy over here where we entered the bay."

"There's another taller hill behind it," Louis said, sketching one in. "When we land, let's work our way through the woods toward it. Hills make good bearings. We can bury the treasure about halfway between the two hills."

"It's spooky on the shore, isn't it?" Lloyd shivered. "If we put more swamp in there, it will frighten away anyone else who might come."

Louis drew in more swamp. "Pirates don't frighten easily, mate. But you can have the swamp. We had better have more hills, too. We'll want to post lookouts. There is a lot of traffic on the sea around here."

Lloyd's eyes devoured the map. He could see longboats swarming with pirates. He could smell the heavy undergrowth of the swampland. He could hear the sounds of pirates coming through the woods. Lloyd picked up a pencil and drew some lines near Mizzenmast Hill.

"A cave," he explained. "It will be dry, and a safe place to hide."

"Good boy," said Louis. "Just in time, too, because here comes

a ship!" Louis quickly sketched a ship with full sails in the corner of the map. "Their lookout has his spyglass aimed in our direction."

"They can't see us here in the cave, but won't they see our ship anchored in the bay?" Lloyd was worried.

"We'll have to wait and see." They both leaned closely over the desk.

"It's time for tea," a voice at the door rang out and made them both jump.

Lloyd's mother, Fanny, had come home. She did not notice how she had startled her husband and her son. She was busy taking off her wet raincoat and patting her damp hair.

"Terrible weather," she said.

Fanny came over to the desk. "What are you two doing now?"

Louis laughed. "In our own way, we are as waterlogged as you are, my dear." He winked at Lloyd. "Time out! Come along."

He put one arm around his wife, and the other around the boy. The three walked across the room while Fanny spoke again of the weather.

Lloyd did not hear. He was thousands of miles from Scotland, breathlessly imagining a ship drawing nearer and nearer to the swampy shore of an island in the Spanish Main.

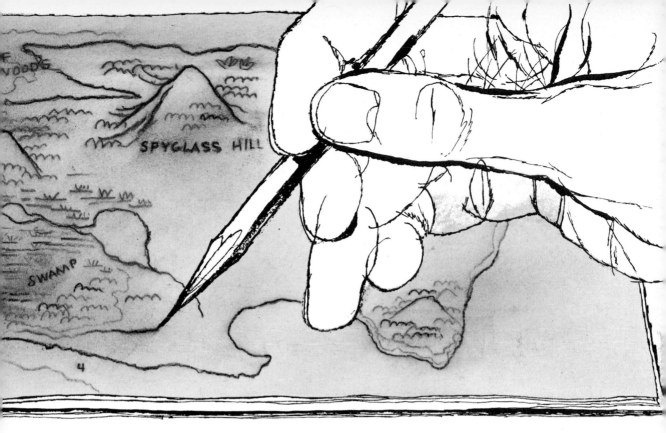

Through the rest of that long wet August, Louis and Lloyd filled in more details on their map.

The rains continued, but now Lloyd did not even notice the weather. Though he was housebound, he was enchanted by the new game. He was entirely absorbed in watching the map fill up with new adventures.

Then before he realized it, moving day arrived.

The house was in an uproar, with everyone rushing around, doors slamming, trunks being dragged out, suitcases crammed with belongings, books and papers thrust helter-skelter into any boxes that were handy.

Within twenty-four hours, the family was ready to leave.

Lloyd, in the midst of all the excitement on that last morning, went to his stepfather's desk to get his beloved map. There was a jumble of papers and notebooks in the top drawer. But the map was not among them!

Lloyd began to search frantically through the desk. It was no use. The map was nowhere to be found!

"Lloyd!" It was Fanny calling. "I need you to carry some of these boxes downstairs. Lloyd, where are you?"

Lloyd kept pulling out drawer after drawer, hunting through the masses of papers.

"Lloyd!"

"I *have* to find it. It must be here," Lloyd muttered, almost in tears. "Oh, where is it? Where is it?"

"Lloyd!"

"Shiver my sides, this time she means it! Coming, mother!"

He ran up the stairs. "Please let me find Louis first," he begged. "The map's gone. We can't go without the map. We just can't!"

"Why do you need it so badly?" Fanny asked. "It's just a drawing. Can't you make another?"

Lloyd shook his head. "It wouldn't be the same. We've got to have it."

"Well, get Louis to help you hunt. Only hurry. The carriage is almost ready. I have just a few more things to carry down."

Lloyd ran down the hall. He was panting with excitement and anxiety. The room that belonged to Louis was bare of all his belongings. At first, Lloyd thought no one was there, but when he looked over at the window, he saw Louis watching the rain.

Lloyd ran to him. "Louis! Oh, Louis! I can't find the map anywhere. Please help me look for it. We can't go without it!"

Louis looked away from the window and grinned down at the worried boy. "We can draw another, you know."

"It would never be the same," Lloyd insisted. "Why, every single mark and picture on it means something. You know that. When we look at the map, we can remember every adventure we've made up about it and every character we've met there on the island. I want them all to go with us."

Louis put his hand on the boy's shoulder. "So you feel that way about it, too!" He smiled, "I was teasing you just now. Our map is the most important piece of paper in this house. It was the first thing I went to get when we started to pack."

He pulled his other hand from behind his back and waved the map triumphantly under Lloyd's nose.

They *were* going to take the map with them. Fanny watched from the doorway, shaking her head. But there was just the trace of a smile on her face.

Louis in this story was Robert Louis Balfour Stevenson, a writer and poet who wrote some of the most exciting stories in English literature. Lloyd was Lloyd Osbourne, Fanny's son and Louis' stepson.

The map that Louis and Lloyd used for their game that rainy summer became far more important than either of them imagined. It was because of that map and the adventures that they made up about the island and the buried pirate treasure that Robert Louis Stevenson was to write one of his most thrilling books. For both the island on the map and the book that Louis wrote were called *Treasure Island*.

More To Read

Robert Louis Stevenson: His Life by Catherine Owens Peare. Published by Holt, Rinehart & Winston, Inc., New York, 1955.

The Lantern Bearer; A Life of Robert Louis Stevenson by James Wood. Published by Pantheon Books, Inc., New York, 1965.

Painting of Robert Louis Stevenson by John Singer Sargent

THE
GREAT
TREASURE
HUNT

BY BETH MARGO

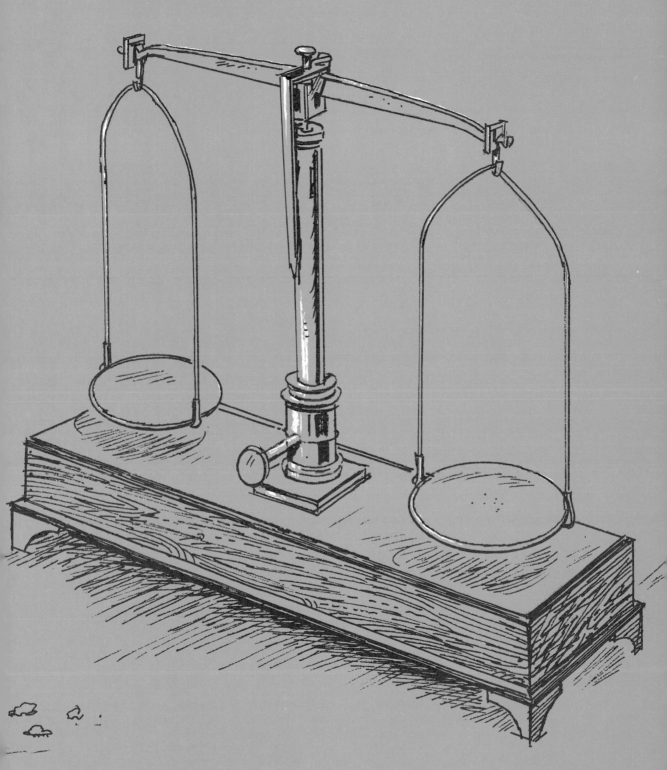

On the evening of January 28, 1848, Captain John Sutter of California closed his account books and sat back with a smile. His dream was coming true. For fourteen years, he had worked hard. Now at last, he was beginning to get results.

His fields stretched for miles around him. His cattle grazed peacefully in the meadow. His Indian helpers tended the budding orchards. Mormons from Salt Lake hammered in the shops of Sutter's Fort, turning out harnesses and wagon wheels for the pioneers who came in covered wagons to California. By March, his new flour mill and sawmill would be finished.

Yes, Captain Sutter felt like a king, a fat smiling king with a gray mustache. He smiled because all was well in his tiny kingdom. And now there were rumors that California might become a state. Who knew how much greater his kingdom might grow?

Suddenly, Sutter heard a loud knocking at the door. He turned toward the door and called out, "Come in!"

A thin man dressed in buckskin, with a brightly colored blanket over his shoulder, stepped into the office and glanced fearfully around. He looked as if someone were after him.

"Good evening, John!" said Captain Sutter.

Sutter couldn't imagine what John Marshall might want now. Why wasn't he in the hills, building the sawmill on the river?

Only yesterday Sutter had sent him the millstones and food to last a whole week. But John Marshall was a strange one—a wanderer and a quarrelsome man. Still, he was a clever mechanic, and good labor was hard to find.

"Are we alone?" John Marshall whispered.

Sutter nodded.

"Lock the door, then," said Marshall.

"Why? No one comes here but my clerk."

"Lock it!"

Sutter shrugged and turned the lock. "What's the matter, John?" he asked.

"Bring me something to make a scale."

The man is crazy, Sutter thought, but I may as well humor him.

"I'll get a scale from the shop," he said.

When he came back with it, Marshall pulled a rag from his pocket and began to unroll it. Just then a clerk passed through the office. Marshall quickly stuffed the rag back into his pocket and glared at Sutter.

"You see?" he raged. "There are spies everywhere! Why didn't

"It's gold!"

you lock the door again when you came back with the scale?"

Feeling angry with Marshall, Sutter dismissed the clerk and locked the door. Perhaps he should have listened to those who said Marshall was crazy.

"Very well, then, for goodness sakes show me your big mystery!"

Slowly, Marshall unrolled the cloth and held it out to Sutter. Peering down, Sutter saw dull-yellow flakes mixed with rock and sand.

"Gold!" cried Marshall, his eyes wide and gleaming. "I found it while I was digging out near the sawmill. The people at the mill laughed at me, but I know it's real gold."

Sutter took the cloth and shook the flakes about, staring at them with interest. "Let's weigh it," he said. "We'll see how it compares with silver."

They found out that the flakes were heavier than silver. Since Sutter knew that gold weighs more than silver, he thought these flakes could be gold.

"You see?" said Marshall.

"Maybe," said Sutter. "We'll try the acid test."

He touched the flakes with acid. Nothing happened.

"It has to be gold. Acid won't eat through it. Now do you believe me?" asked John Marshall.

"I believe you," said Sutter. "But I'll come up to the mill to see for myself."

Sutter went with Marshall to the sawmill. He looked at the nuggets the men had found. He took his knife and dug yellow flakes from the rocky crevices of the millrace. He frowned at the nuggets in his handkerchief. He would have a ring made from this, the first California gold. But he was not happy as he put the gold in his pocket.

If the news spread, people would flock to hunt for gold. His orchards and fields would be destroyed. His sawmill and flour mill would never be finished. All the years he had spent working on this land, his own land, would be useless!

He turned to speak to his workers. "I must ask you a favor," he said to the men. "Promise me that you'll say nothing about this for six weeks. I will pay you double wages if you finish the mills. Hunt for all the gold you

"We have gold!"

"You must be plumb loco!"

want, but please don't tell *anyone!* Just give me six weeks."

The men all promised. They went on building the mill and hunting for gold in their spare time. Then, one day one of Sutter's drivers, who didn't know about the gold, found some children playing with yellow pebbles.

"We have gold!" they told him.

"You must be plumb loco!" the driver laughed.

Their mother came out of the cabin and shook her apron at him. "Run along, don't tease them!" she scolded. "Of course they have gold. They found it for themselves."

The driver stopped laughing. He picked up one of the nuggets and quickly drove his team all the way back to Sutter's Fort. He rushed into Sam Brannan's store and slammed his fist on the counter. "Service!" he shouted.

"Hold on! Where are your silver dollars?"

"Who needs silver?" the driver shouted. "I have gold!" He threw the nugget down on the counter.

Brannan didn't believe him. They went over to have Captain Sutter settle the argument. Sutter sighed and nodded his head.

"It's true, Sam, but just give me a little time. I must have my mills finished. If the word gets out now, everything will be ruined."

Sam promised, but he began to do a lot of thinking and planning. If enough people came to hunt for gold, he could make a fortune selling them supplies from his store.

When the workmen finished the mills, they laid down their tools and scampered off to the mountain streams to hunt for gold.

"Gold! Gold on Sutter's land!"

Sam Brannan kept the secret until May. Then he went shouting down the streets of San Francisco, waving a bag of nuggets high over his head for everyone to see.

"Gold! Gold on Sutter's land!"

The people of San Francisco left their shops and rushed off to the gold country.

The secret was out. The great treasure hunt was on.

And that was the end of John Sutter's dream.

324

Most people would have been delirious with joy to have gold discovered on their land. But John Sutter was not interested in gold. He had spent many years dreaming of the day when his mills and fields would be ready. The discovery of gold destroyed his dream just when it was about to come true.

There was no one to work the mills. There was no one to harvest the wheat. There was no one to pick the ripened fruit from the orchards. Everyone had gone to look for gold.

The next year, 1849, the Gold Rush was on. Treasure hunters came to Sutter's Fort from all parts of the world. Men stole his cattle, broke up his shops, even stole the millstones from the flour mill and the cannons and bells from the Fort.

Gold had opened a great new state, but it had crushed John Sutter's little fairytale kingdom in the sun.

Captain Sutter died a poor and bitter man. He died without ever knowing that it was not gold that would make California rich in the long run, but orchards, vineyards, shops, and mills like the ones at Sutter's Fort.

Sutter's Fort, as restored, in Sacramento, California

More To Read

The California Gold Rush by American Heritage. Published by American Heritage Publishing Company, Inc., New York, 1961.

The First Book of the California Gold Rush by Walter Havighurst. Published by Franklin Watts, Inc., New York, 1962.

A DESPERATE RISK

Four young rangers crouched behind a clump of bushes on a prairie hilltop. The rangers were as silent as statues. Their faces were grim. Yet the long procession of Indian warriors, squaws, dogs, and ponies they were watching on the plain below seemed as gay and comical as a circus parade of clowns.

The Indian warriors had dressed up in long-tailed, black frock coats. Then they had wrapped strips of silk and satin tightly around their stomachs. Some of them wore stovepipe hats, decorated with streamers of ribbon.

The Indian ponies wore big bows of red, blue, orange, and

BY ROBERT WEST HOWARD

pink calico that fluttered in the wind like giant butterflies.

The squaws paraded alongside with flowered and checkered bedspreads wrapped over their shoulders.

Even the dogs jogging beside the squaws had collars of gold and jewels.

The four rangers hidden on the hilltop could not smile at this clownish procession. Far to the south, smoke still curled from the towns these Comanches had looted and burned. Some people, walking behind the squaws, were captured women and children who were being carried off to slavery in the northern deserts. And following the whole procession was a huge herd made up of horses the Indians had stolen along the way. This was the worst Indian attack there had ever been in the Republic of Texas. Somehow, the Indians had to be stopped.

The tallest of the young rangers dropped to his stomach and began to crawl back toward the gully where their ponies were hidden. The others followed him, single file, wriggling so carefully that not even a bush quivered.

Safe in the gully, the tall leader stood up, brushed the dust from his jeans and leaned against his pony. Revolvers dangled at his hips. A long-barreled mountaineer's rifle was strapped behind his pony's saddle.

"The way I see it, those redskins will be just about crossing the Plum Creek by the morning after next," the tall ranger said.

"Just what I was thinking, Ben," one of the rangers replied.

Ben went on, "If we can get word into San Antonio tonight and start some troops moving, we just might be able to stop them at Plum Creek."

"It must be a hundred miles to San Antonio," the other man murmured. "Then it's another sixty miles to Plum Creek. Do you want us all to go?"

"We can't take the chance." Ben shook his head. "Barney, you and Alsey follow the Comanches. I'll take Archie and ride on toward San Antonio. If the Indians are still headed the same way tomorrow morning, make a break for Plum Creek. We'll meet you there the next day in the willows near the crossing. Good luck."

Ben swung up on his pony as he spoke. He snapped his right hand to his hat brim in a salute and rode off. Archie rode after him.

Ben realized that if the Comanches succeeded in this raid other Indian tribes would organize raiding parties, too. Ben knew that he had to stop the Comanches now, or there would be Indian wars in Texas for years to come.

But he also knew that he and Archie couldn't ride to San Antonio at full speed. Their ponies had already carried them a long way during the past week. A headlong race now might kill the ponies. So the two rangers rode at a steady jog and stopped every hour or two to rest the ponies.

The positions of the stars told them it was early the next morning when they saw a series of campfires flickering up ahead. Ben knew they were coming to the town of Seguin, which was on the way to San Antonio.

The families of Seguin should have been asleep! The campfires could only mean that news of the Comanche raid had spread, and the people had prepared themselves for an attack.

Ben and Archie jogged cautiously across the prairie until they were within a half mile of the fires. Then Ben threw back his head and put all his lung power into a high, terrible battle scream that he had learned from some old Indian fighters. "Waah Hooheeee!"

A sentry's challenge barked from the darkness off to their left. "Halt! Keep your hands up!"

"We're rangers," Ben called. "We have news about the Comanches."

"WE'RE RANGERS . . ."

"Advance and be recognized, rangers," the sentry shouted.

Ten minutes later, Ben and Archie were unsaddling their ponies beside a campfire. Ben told an army officer what he and the other rangers had seen from the hilltop. He reported that the Comanches were marching toward Plum Creek.

"We judge they'll get to Plum Creek sometime tomorrow forenoon," Ben concluded. "There are more than five hundred warriors. But if we can get enough Texans up there ahead of them, we can give those Indians a real hot time of it."

Ben worked on his pony as he talked, gently rubbing down her sweaty flanks and examining her legs for bruises or thorns. Only when he was sure she was fit for a night's graze did he settle down with the group of officers for discussion of plans.

Messengers were sent out to gather enough men to face the Indians at Plum Creek. Every town on the frontier had kept bands of armed men on the alert since the first Comanche raid.

Within an hour, Ben and Archie were stretched out, asleep on their saddle blankets while the messengers galloped toward Gonzales, Austin, and San Antonio with orders to troops there to ride hard to Plum Creek.

The next morning Ben and Archie were among a group of almost two hundred Texans who crouched in the bushes along Plum Creek, silently watching for the first sign of the Comanches.

Two shadowy figures came riding toward them.

The Texans tensed and took aim with their guns and rifles.

Suddenly, Ben recognized the two men approaching. They were Barney and Alsey, the rangers he had sent to scout the Comanches. "Don't shoot," Ben ordered. "They're rangers."

As they neared the bushes, Barney shouted, "The Indians are about three miles back."

"CHARGE!"

"We're over here on your left," Ben called. "Come on over. We've got a little surprise party lined up."

Mutters of command sounded down the line, followed by the squeak of saddle straps being tightened, the tap-tap of bullets ramming into rifles, and the snap of revolvers cocking.

Ben beckoned to Barney and Alsey as they splashed across the creek. The four rangers shook hands. Then Ben whispered a plan. "When the Indians get close to the creek, we'll try to surprise them with a sudden charge. Then, when I give the word, we four will turn and head for the herd of horses the Comanches stole from the settlers. If we can get those horses to stampede into the Indians, we'll win this fight."

"It just might work," Barney said.

Just then the Comanches came into view.

Hands tense on reins, the Texans sat waiting for several minutes.

Finally, the command rang out, "Charge!"

The line of Texans galloped across the creek. But the Comanches must have heard the command. Their warriors were already gathering into battle lines, and fitting arrows to their bows. The Comanche war chief put on his feather headdress and rode alone toward the Texans. He waved his lance and chanted a death challenge in a high-pitched voice.

The four rangers spurred their ponies. The animals raced ahead of the rest of the charging Texans.

Ben dropped his reins, whipped his rifle to his shoulder, took quick aim, and fired.

The Comanche war chief gave a twisting leap, screamed, and fell to the ground.

"Now!" Ben yelled. "Head for the horses!"

The four rangers turned and rode toward the huge herd of stolen horses. The Comanches made no move to stop them, but raced instead toward the other charging Texans.

A hundred yards from the horse herd the four rangers suddenly reined their ponies to a stop. They waved their hats over their heads and let go with a war scream, "Waah Hooheeee!"

The lead horses of the herd whinnied, reared, and turned in fright. Their hoofs slashed against the horses behind them.

The rangers charged another fifty yards, and reined their ponies again. Off went their hats. "Waah Hooheeee!" The war cry echoed once more.

The horse herd became a whinnying, pawing bedlam.

Once again the rangers rode until the horse herd was directly between the rangers and the Indians.

"Waah Hooheeee!" The scream rose a third time.

Every horse in the herd turned and charged blindly toward the Comanche warriors.

When the Comanches saw the herd of charging horses, they scattered in all directions.

Within fifteen minutes, the Comanches were galloping toward their homeland. The Texans were rounding up the horse herd, and piling up the stolen goods. The rangers began untying the rescued women and children.

Thanks to Ben and the other rangers, the Comanches had been stopped.

Ben in this story was Ben McCullough. He and Barney and Archie and Alsey were members of the Texas Rangers, a band of men that had been formed to protect the young Republic of Texas.

The Texans won the victory of Plum Creek on August 12, 1840. Six years later, Texas voted to become a state in the U.S.A. But that did not mean an end for the gallant Texas Rangers. They have served as scouts and policemen on the Texas frontier ever since.

Ben McCullough became one of their great heroes. His scouting duties enabled the Americans to win at least one of the great battles in the War with Mexico. Ben was promoted to captain and then major in the Rangers. He served as a U.S. Marshal, too, and was a Brigadier General of the Southern forces during the Civil War. But many people agree that at no time in his life did Ben display greater wisdom and bravery than he did when he outrode and outsmarted the deadly Comanches and won peace for the Texas frontier at Plum Creek.

A Texas Ranger as he looks today▶

More To Read

Big Foot Wallace of the Texas Rangers by Shannon Garst. Published by Julian Messner, New York, 1951.

Texas by Allan Carpenter. Published by Childrens Press, Inc., Chicago, 1965.

HOW THE KING WAS TRICKED

By Virginia Robinson

"I shall not take part in your war games," the King of Ithaca shouted to his men. "No! I shall never fight again, not even in games."

The men looked at one another. Had their king gone crazy?

"I won't fight, ever again," the king bellowed. "I shall spend the rest of my life here on the island of Ithaca with my family. We shall live in peace in this great palace."

His beard twitched as he walked among his men through the palace courtyard. Suddenly, he reached down and picked up a huge stone. He hurled it through the air and sent it smashing into the courtyard wall, twenty feet away.

"I shall not fight because I am too weak, and I can barely walk," he said. Then he began to laugh.

At first, the men stood in shocked silence. And then they began to laugh, too. The men pressed forward, enjoying the joke of their king, who pretended to be so weak he could not lift a finger and yet could hurl a stone that no one else could even lift, twenty feet into a wall.

The king pushed his way through them and returned to the side of his wife, Penelope.

He turned to his men. "I say to you, have your games. Wrestle! Play hard, so you may work hard. But I shall not fight again—not even in play. I have met my match—here!"

He lifted a baby boy from the arms of his wife and held the child high. The child grabbed his father's finger. The king shouted, "I must save my strength to wrestle with my son."

The men applauded, stamped their feet, and cheered as they moved out of the courtyard and into the meadow to begin their games.

The king watched them go with a smile on his face. "Nothing will make me go to war again," he repeated to Penelope who stood beside him.

Penelope looked away. "You say that!" she said, scolding him gently. "But what of your promise?"

"Yes, my promise," the king said. He thought of the day many years ago when he had promised to defend Helen, the most beautiful woman in Greece, if ever she or her husband asked for help.

But no woman was so beautiful to him as his Penelope! He put one arm around her, his other arm gently cradling his son. "Helen is safe. Her husband is a strong man and can well defend her."

"That is true," said Penelope. "But I wish you had not given your promise!"

"I shall not fight again," vowed the king. "There is nothing that will take me away from you and our child. Besides, there is the warning of the gods."

Penelope's great dark eyes took fear as if a sword were suddenly thrust to her throat. "The gods? Do you mean that the gods have spoken to you through an oracle?"

"Yes. They have said that if I should leave the island of Ithaca to go to war, I would not return for twenty years. And that is why I never want to fight again," said the king.

"No!" cried Penelope, looking away. "It is—" She looked in fear down the road.

The king glanced at the road. He saw a man running toward them as swiftly as if a fire burned at his heels. "It is—what?" he asked his wife, a harsh note in his voice.

"It is as if I hear the gods laughing when you say that," said Penelope. She shivered.

The running figure came closer.

"There is nothing to fear in Ithaca," said the king. "You see only one of our shepherds coming toward us."

"And behind him?" asked Penelope, drawing closer to her husband again. "Who travels behind the shepherd?"

The king had no answer, for he saw a traveler following the shepherd. The jaw behind his great beard tightened, and a wild light came into his eyes.

Now the sound of running feet came to their ears. They watched as the shepherd burst through the palace gate and came panting and staggering to the ground before them.

"You bring news?" asked the king through tight lips.

"What do you have to say to me? Speak!"

"My king," gasped the shepherd. "The woman Helen has been kidnapped by the Trojans. Her husband calls for your help to make ready for war. The traveler who follows behind me is coming to make you keep your promise to Helen."

The king listened to the shepherd's words. He looked at his wife and saw the look of fear on her face. He looked down at the child he held in his arms. He did not want to leave. But he had promised to defend Helen. And yet he remembered the oracle's terrible warning. Twenty years! What could he do? Was there some way he could stay with his wife and child without seeming to break his promise? Suddenly he had an idea. He turned to the shepherd.

"You bring news, eh, shepherd? And what do you have to say? Speak, shepherd, for your voice comes from far away, and I hear nothing. Speak! You cannot? You have nothing to say to me, shepherd?" The king's voice grew louder and louder as the traveler entered the gate.

"Take this child, woman." The king thrust his son at Penelope.

The child began to cry.

"Take the child!" cried the king. "It is my time for the fields. I must plow! I must plow!"

The king sprang from the steps and ran through the gates toward the meadow where the men were busy with their war games.

"I must plow!" cried the king, his great voice resounding in the distance.

He seized a wooden-handled plow and turning, he ran a deep furrow across the road and back before the astounded eyes of the traveler.

The traveler turned to Penelope. "Has the great king gone crazy? The war is lost if he cannot fight with us."

"I must plow!" cried the king, and he ran the plow through the meadow, while clumps of dirt and stones flew from his path. All the while he kept thinking, I must make them believe that I have gone crazy. A crazy man would not be expected to keep his promise.

The men had stopped their games and had joined the group in front of the palace. They stared at their king in wonder.

"I must plow," cried the king, swerving back toward the palace. He ran straight into the palace wall.

"He must be out of his mind!" cried the traveler, hiding behind a large rock. "And yet I must remember that this is a shrewd and crafty king." He looked at Penelope and the shepherd.

"He *is* out of his mind!" cried the shepherd, sinking to his knees in the road and crying as if his heart would break. "Our king is out of his mind."

"Out of his mind," said Penelope softly. She began to weep, and her tears fell on the face of her child.

The king smashed the plow into the wall again and again until he finally burst through the wall and into the palace gardens.

He ran the plow through the gardens and out of the gate, heading back toward the meadow, digging a deep furrow in the earth. Then he turned the plow and headed back to the garden, straight for the traveler.

I think my plan is working, thought the king. They seem to believe me.

But then something happened! The king saw the traveler grab the baby from Penelope's arms and place the child straight in his path.

"I do not believe he is crazy," shouted the traveler. "If I am right, he will turn the plow from the path of his child."

"No! No!" cried Penelope in terror.

My son, thought the king, my beautiful son.

He turned the plow away from the child.

The traveler again placed the child in the path of the plow.

The king again turned away.

A third time, and the result was the same.

The king stopped and stood with his great head bowed.

"It is no use," he said softly. "You have tricked me. I was foolish to think that I could break my promise."

Penelope stretched out her arms to her husband and cried. "It is the will of the gods, my king. You know that as well as I do. Only evil will befall us if we go against their will."

The king came slowly back to the group in front of the palace.

"The gods say that I shall wander for twenty years," he moaned. "I shall miss the youth of my wife. I shall miss the youth of my son. It will be twenty years before I return home. But I am indeed wrong to think that I could forget my pledge of honor. I made a promise, and I shall keep it. I shall fight for as long as I am needed. It is the will of the gods."

Ulysses, the King of Ithaca in this story, was one of the heroes of ancient Greece. His many thrilling adventures are told in two poems, the *Iliad* and the *Odyssey*, written by Homer, a Greek poet.

Ulysses kept his promise and went to war. The war lasted for ten years. Finally, the Trojans were defeated and Helen was saved. On his return trip Ulysses' ship was blown off course, and it took him another ten years to find his way home. The warning of the oracle had come true. Ulysses did not return home for twenty years.

The story of Ulysses is part of the folklore of ancient Greece. No one knows whether Ulysses really lived. But the stories about him have lasted for thousands of years.

More To Read

The Adventures of Odysseus and the Tale of Troy by Padraic Colum. Published by The Macmillan Company. New York, 1918.

The Iliad and the Odyssey of Homer retold by Alfred J. Church. Published by the Macmillan Company, New York, 1964.

Afraid to Move

"Booker! Stop daydreaming and start working."

"What? Oh, thanks, John."

John laughed, "Your mind must have been miles away. What were you dreaming about this time?"

"School!" Booker jabbed at a mound of coal with his pick. "Do you think we'll ever get a chance to go to school, John?"

"Shhhh! Start working, Booker!" John whispered his warning —but too late. The mine boss had come storming over.

Booker trembled as the man towered above him.

"I've had enough of this!" the mine boss bellowed. "Booker, you've been jabbering like a jay bird all afternoon. I'll break this up. You, John! Come with me. I'm taking you and the other miners into a new section of the mine. Booker can stay and finish this digging."

By Lillie Patterson

"Please!" John begged. "Let me stay and help my brother. He works hard. Honest, he does. I'll stay late tonight to make up for the time we lost. Please!"

"Get your pick and come with us," the boss ordered.

"But he'll get lost trying to find us. He doesn't know his way in the mines yet. I have to look out for him," John pleaded.

The mine boss pushed John ahead of him. "Booker, you join us when you are finished here."

Booker was left alone.

He began digging as fast as his young arms could lift the pick and bring it down again.

Banging his pick against a big lump of coal, Booker whispered, "I hate this mine. I hate it!" Tears of frustration choked his voice.

And then Booker's chin jutted out in the stubborn way it always did when he made up his mind to do something. "I'm going to leave this old mine some day and go to school," he said aloud. "And after I go to school, I'll be a teacher. I'll teach everybody, even the old folks. I'll build ma a fine home, and she won't have to work so hard, and—"

Booker brought his mind back to his work. He finished digging the pile of coal and set out to find John and the other miners.

He carefully adjusted his miner's lamp so he could see better.

Booker then put his pick on his shoulder and started off in the direction the miners had taken. He walked for a time, then stopped. Now, he wondered, which way shall I turn?

He listened for the sound of voices or the clank of picks. There was only silence.

Booker turned and walked for a time in the opposite direction. Still he could hear no sounds. He cupped his hands to his mouth and called, "Hello! Hello!"

No answer.

Booker knew that he was lost. The more he walked, the more he seemed to be going around in circles. And being lost in the mines was like being lost in a huge, dark forest. He became frightened.

"John!" Booker called desperately. "Where are you?"

There was only the darkness and the silence.

Then suddenly Booker stood stiff with horror. His little lamp flickered and sputtered, flickered and sputtered—then the light went out. Booker was left in blackness.

"Oh, no!" he groaned. "What will I do now?"

Booker dropped to his knees and crouched there in the blackness, trembling with fear. He was afraid to move. He was afraid to stay in one spot. This was worse than just being lost. This was like being all alone in the whole world.

"Help! Help!" Booker called weakly.

Still there was only the silence and the darkness of the coal mines.

Booker didn't move for a long time. His heart kept thumping with fright. Every now and then he called out, but got no answer. At last, a faint, rustling sound caught his attention. He listened. Was a miner coming?

No! A big rat scurried across Booker's toes. He shuddered and curled his body into a ball. After a time he raised his head and called as loud as he could, "Hey! It's me—Booker. I'm lost!"

Crash!

As though in answer, a loud crashing sound echoed from somewhere in the mines.

Falling slate!

Booker shivered and curled up even tighter. Suppose there were a big piece of slate above him, waiting to fall and bash his head in?

Booker stayed as still as a lump of coal for what seemed like hours. No one came. Finally, he got up enough courage to stand. I've got to find the others, he told himself. I must!

Boom!

Booker dropped to the ground again. An explosion this time! How close by was the explosion? Booker wondered. Suppose— just suppose—the men began blasting nearby? No one knew he was there.

On hands and knees he began crawling. Dragging his pick along, inch by inch, he moved, carefully feeling his way.

Then another thought brought even greater panic. He had lost track of the hours. Suppose it was closing time? The others might think that he had gone home. What if they left him to spend the night in the mine—all alone?

Booker crawled even faster. "John! John! Come find me!"

Suddenly, a pinpoint of light flickered far ahead in the darkness. It was followed by another light and another. Booker stopped and held his breath. Was he dreaming? No! He heard the crunching of footsteps.

He jumped up and began running toward the light. "Here I am! Wait for me!"

"Booker?" John shouted.

"I'm coming!" Booker called, his voice ringing through the mines. "I'm coming!"

Booker, the young boy in this story, was Booker T. Washington, a famous American educator. Booker was born a slave. After the slaves were freed, Booker and his family moved to West Virginia where he went to work in the coal mines.

This incident took place in 1868, when Booker was only twelve years old. Booker's dream came true. He left the mines and went to school. Later he became a teacher and organized Tuskegee Institute, a school for Negroes, in Alabama. He was able to give thousands of his people a chance to get a good education. Today, his school is considered one of the finest in the United States.

Booker spent his lifetime helping to improve the lives of Negroes. No list of great Americans is complete without the name of Booker T. Washington.

More To Read

Lift Every Voice by Benjamin Quarles and Dorothy Sterling. Published by Doubleday & Company, Inc., New York, 1965.

"The Building Will Collapse!"

By Jill Moore Marx

"This could be one of the most interesting buildings ever built," the official said, studying the blueprints spread out on his desk in the office of the Wisconsin Industrial Commission. Then he looked at the architect seated opposite him. "But I'm afraid we can't give you a license to build it."

The architect's fingers tightened on the handle of his gold-tipped cane. He stared at the official. "Why not?"

"As you well know, my job is to make sure that no office building or factory goes up here in Racine unless we are sure that it will be safe," the official replied. "Your plan for this building is remarkable. I like your ideas for the offices and the workrooms. I think your plan for an indoor parking lot, a theater, and a

sports area is especially good. What troubles me is the shape of the columns that you've designed to support the ceilings."

The official picked up one of the blueprints. "According to this, your columns are only nine inches wide at the base. And they'll be made of concrete, right?"

"That's right," replied the architect. "What about it?"

"The building laws in this state say that concrete columns with nine-inch bases must not be more than six feet high. Your columns are twenty-four feet high. That means they should be at least thirty-six inches wide at the base. Otherwise, the building will collapse!"

The architect banged his gold-tipped cane on the floor. "My columns are more than strong enough to hold up the ceilings," he said. "I designed them with narrow bases because I was thinking about the people who will have to work in the building. If I use wide columns, there won't be enough space for people to move about. My columns will give everyone plenty of room."

"That's all very well," the official said. "But I still think your columns are too weak." He began to scribble some numbers on a sheet of paper. "Look here, each of your columns will have to support *twelve tons*. My figures show that they couldn't support more than *two* tons without cracking. I'm sorry, but at that rate the building would be unsafe. I can't give you a license to build."

The architect frowned. "Sir, my columns *can* support this building. Run a test on one of the columns, and I'm sure we'll both be satisfied. You'll know that the building will be safe, and I can get on with my work."

"All right," the official agreed. "We'll set up one of your columns on the building lot. If it can hold twelve tons, you can go ahead and start building. But if the column collapses, I'll never allow you to put up the building in this city."

In the days that followed, the newspapers were full of guesses about the outcome of the test. Many reporters believed that the column would collapse. They said the building was doomed.

The people of Racine were anxious. They hoped to see the beautiful building in their city. Many of them were looking forward to working in it.

Finally, the day for the test came. The building lot filled with so many people that the police had to put up barricades to protect the spectators. The official from the Wisconsin Industrial Commission was there. The contractor was there. The people who had hired the architect to design their building were there.

And the architect was there. It was a rather chilly day in June so the architect wore a shawl about his shoulders. He stood on top of a pile of building materials watching the proceedings through a pair of opera glasses.

An exact copy of the column stood in the middle of the lot. It looked like a gigantic golf tee with its narrow stem and flat round top.

A huge steam shovel swung into action and began to dump gravel and bags of cement on the round top of the column. One ton . . . two tons. The column did not collapse as the official had said it would. It did not even shake. But would it hold twelve tons?

The steam shovel clanked and creaked as it swung back and forth, lifting and dumping more bags of cement and gravel on the top of the column. Six tons . . . seven tons . . . eight tons. The crowd watched in tense silence.

"Well, sir, what do you think of my column now?" the architect asked, lowering his opera glasses.

"Amazing," the official replied. "I can't understand why your column didn't collapse long ago. Only four more tons to go and there isn't even a sign of strain."

The architect smiled and again raised his opera glasses to watch the steam shovel as it piled more weight on his column. Nine tons . . . ten . . . eleven . . . and then twelve!

For a moment, no one said a word. Everyone watched the column and waited. It remained upright and rigid. The column had passed the test! Now the building could be started. A loud cheer rose from the crowd.

The official shook hands with the architect. "I can't believe it," he said. "Your column is a magnificent piece of engineering. Will it hold more weight?"

"Certainly," the architect answered proudly. "Tell the steam shovel operator to keep adding weight until I signal him to stop."

The steam shovel loaded more and more weight on the column . . . sixteen tons, twenty-eight tons . . . forty-two tons, fifty-six tons . . . sixty tons. Still the column stood. Now, at last, small cracks began to appear in the upper part of the column—the widest, but weakest part. The architect raised his hand and signaled the operator to stop. But the architect had proved to everyone's satisfaction that his column was very safe indeed. It had supported five times as much weight as it needed to support before it had shown any sign of weakness.

Frank Lloyd Wright

The architect in this story was Frank Lloyd Wright, one of the greatest architects the world has known. This story took place in 1937 in Racine, Wisconsin. The building, designed by Mr. Wright for S. C. Johnson and Son, Incorporated, has become a famous work of architecture.

Frank Lloyd Wright believed that each building should be designed to fit the needs of the people who would occupy it. Many people thought that his buildings were strange, and they criticized Wright for being different. But his designs started a new style in architecture. Many modern houses, office buildings, and factories are modeled after designs made by Frank Lloyd Wright.

Some of Wright's most famous buildings are the Robie House in Chicago, Illinois; the Guggenheim Museum in New York City; Unity Church in Oak Park, Illinois; and the Larkin Company Administration Building in Buffalo, New York.

More To Read

Frank Lloyd Wright: Rebel in Concrete by Aylesa Forsee. Published by Macrae Smith, Philadelphia, Pa., 1959.

Frank Lloyd Wright: His Life, His Work, His Words by Olgivanna Lloyd Wright. Published by Horizon Press, New York, 1966.

Inside view of the Johnson Administration Building

Outside view of the buildings of S. C. Johnson & Son, Inc. in Racine, Wisconsin

"I Am That Man!"

By Helen Kaye Miller

Pctcr sat on a large coil of rope close to the ship's railing and watched the ocean roll and sparkle in the sun. High above his head, the vessel's huge square sails flapped and billowed in a wind that held steady but was gentler than at any time since the voyage from England began.

He hoped the wind would soon grow stronger to carry him faster to America. Hc strained his eyes to the horizon, but thcrc was no land to see yet. Only wide stretches of blue sky and water.

The fresh, salty air and the hot sun made him drowsy. He became lost in a daydream of what he, a 13-year-old boy from Germany, would do in the new land ahead.

He would go to school, and so would his brothcr and sister when they grew older.

Maybc hc could have all he wanted to eat! It seemed years since he had eaten a really good meal. He closed his eyes and imagined having a platterful of boiled potatoes and juicy roast beef.

Perhaps he could even have new clothes. And he rubbed the familiar worn spot on the knee of his faded green breeches.

"Peter! John Peter!"

Startled, he opened his eyes. His little sister, Anna, was running to him with skirts blowing in the breeze and yellow pigtails bobbing.

"John Peter," she repeated breathlessly, "Mother wants us down below deck. Please hurry!"

It's Father, he thought with a pang of fright, and he leaped

off the rope and took one of Anna's small hands in his. Other travelers looked at them half-curiously as they ran to the hatchway and vanished through it.

Anna tripped on her skirt and tore it as they went down the steep ladder, and Peter clutched at her and held her tightly. "Go easy," he said, and carefully guided her steps to the cargo area below.

Oil lanterns, swaying above them on creaking chains, gave a dim and flickering light to the damp hold, and odors of unwashed bodies and clothing mingled with other unpleasant smells. On this voyage the cargo was people, more than 200 of them jammed together with only their dreams of America to make life bearable.

Peter found it hard to weave his way through the crowds of people standing, sitting, or lying down in every space. But he led Anna as quickly as possible toward a far corner of the hold.

As they squeezed past one last group of travelers, Peter saw his mother and his small brother, Johannes, kneeling beside his sick father, who lay on a thin blanket spread out on the wooden flooring.

His father raised his head slightly and smiled as Peter and Anna approached. How thin Father was, thought Peter, and how uncomfortable he must be on that hard bed. Like so many other passengers, his father had been ill with fever for many days.

Even so, Peter thought how dignified his father looked, with his strong face and thick, wavy hair and beard. But the face looked so pale today. Peter felt a lump come to his throat as his father tried to lift a hand toward him.

Peter reached for the hand with both of his and held it firmly.

"My dear John Peter," said his father, speaking slowly with effort. "You are only 13, and yet you are more man than boy. Very soon you must be ALL man, and show everyone what a fine man you can be."

The lump rose higher in Peter's throat, making it hard to speak, but he managed to answer, "Yes, Father."

Looking from Peter to Anna and then Johannes, their father next turned to their mother, saying, "Johanna, my darling, we have three fine children, do we not? Let them each kiss me. Then I must rest."

She nodded and waved the three forward. They stooped, kissed their father, then clung to one another.

Peter ached to know the truth about his father, but he knew this was not the time to discuss it. His mother's eyes were bright with unshed tears as she gave him a small, understanding smile and said, "Son, take your brother and sister to the captain. He has promised to give you food and sleeping quarters. I will send word or come to you later." She began to stroke her husband's forehead tenderly, murmuring words of comfort.

Johannes and Anna followed closely behind Peter to the main deck, and then forward to the captain's bridge. Johannes was sobbing; and, even without looking, Peter knew that Anna was silently crying. He held himself tense so as not to cry, also. Harsh as the truth was to face, he knew his father was dying.

The captain saw them coming and called out a greeting. Very soon he helped Johannes forget his tears by lifting the boy high enough to reach his short arms to the ship's wheel.

"Oh, look at me, Peter!" the little boy said. "I'm steering us to America!"

Captain Andrews winked at Peter, and Peter made an effort to wink back like one grown man sharing a joke with another. He did not feel like a man. He was a boy, and when he had his turn at the wheel he became as excited as Johannes. How powerful one felt guiding a great ocean-going vessel!

Peter's fears for his father returned as he glanced at Anna, who huddled against Johannes standing there sadly. At the same time, he felt Captain Andrews' big hand on his shoulder, and heard him say, "If I know boys and girls, they are always hungry. Let's visit Cook."

Calling to one of his officers to take over the wheel, the captain led the youngsters below deck to the galley.

Bending over a table was a short, stocky man who was cutting thick slices from a large chunk of dried beef. This was Cook, and Peter liked him from the moment he turned around with a grizzled grin, his blue eyes flashing.

After a few whispered words to Cook, the captain waved at

them and left. Soon, Peter, Johannes, and Anna were munching dried beef and hard, flat biscuits. The food and Cook's gruff, jolly voice as he served it made them feel better.

Later, they were given a sleeping place in a small cabin off the galley. Johannes and Anna each had a bed. But Peter had something he thought was better. It was a rope hammock that had been hard to climb into, but that held him snugly and swung with the motion of the ship.

Neither of the younger children was crying, now; but as he peered through the knotted rope of his swinging bed, Peter could see tears caught in Anna's thick lashes as she slept. He sighed deeply and fell asleep himself.

It was nearly dawn when he felt a touch on his hair. Instantly, he awoke. His mother stood beside him, her face chalk-white as she motioned to him. He felt the same kind of fear that he had when Anna had called to him earlier that day. But this time the fear raced his heart even stronger. He climbed out of the hammock and went with his mother to the deck.

She found a railing and leaned against it for a few silent moments. Then she turned and hugged him closely. "Oh, my dear Peter," she murmured, "your father has gone from us!"

Peter threw his arms around his mother's waist, and tears burst from his eyes. He did not speak. He could not.

They held onto one another for a long time. Then his mother moved far enough away to look deeply into his eyes, saying, "Remember the last words your father spoke to you. 'You are only 13,' he said, 'yet you are more man than boy.' You must be a good and strong man."

Peter swallowed hard and nodded.

Side by side, they waited for the arrival of the sun as dark water splashed against the heavy ship and salt spray hit them.

Peter's dreams of what America would be like for him were different ones, now. As he walked about the ship either alone or with Johannes and Anna, and as he ate and slept, his day visions and his night dreams were filled with what he must now do.

No longer could he think of being a schoolboy in America. He must become at least self-supporting.

A few days after his father had been buried at sea, he was staring over a railing thinking of his father when Captain Andrews came up to him.

"Peter," he said, "I know you have been wondering what you will do in the new land, and I've been thinking about that, too.

"I know a fine man in this New York Colony where you're going. His name is William Bradford, and he is in the printing trade. If I can convince him to take you on as an apprentice, you'll be learning a good trade that can bring you a steady income. If you and your mother wish me to, I will talk to Mr. Bradford as soon as we reach port."

"Oh, thank you, sir!" exclaimed Peter. "May we please tell Mother right away?"

A sense of relief flooded upon him at that moment and stayed with him through the sighting of land . . . the stepping onto the new continent of America . . . and through the details of settling the family. At last, he and his mother stood before a small shop along a cobblestoned street in New York Colony.

Peter looked up at the sign that read, "William Bradford, Printer." For the first time in days, he felt a tingle of excitement, along with a faint worry: Will he want me as his apprentice?

Peter and his mother went inside the ink-smelling shop. Peter's eyes traveled from a desk cluttered with paper and ink-pots to some long tables with boxes on them, and on to the back. There, a man as tall as his father stood behind the jutting angles of a strange-looking machine made of wooden posts and slabs.

Seeing Peter and his mother the man called out, "I'll be right with you!" Peter saw him turn a handle on the machine that made some of its parts move together with a clatter. With another turn of the handle, he made the parts separate. From a surface near the center of the machine, he then lifted a sheet of paper which he carried as he walked toward Peter, saying, "If this is to be my new apprentice, here's a first lesson."

Showing Peter that one side of the paper had large black letters on it, he said, "This is a printed page, and if you're chosen as my apprentice, you'll be printing many of them."

Peter looked at it and then up at Mr. Bradford with a hopeful smile. Would he be accepted?

He heard his mother say, "Yes, this is my son, of whom Captain Andrews has spoken to you. May we sign the necessary papers so that his apprenticeship will begin?"

Mr. Bradford placed his head to one side and looked down at Peter in a stern way, although his eyes did not look stern at all. It was an expression Peter remembered in his father's eyes.

"Well, there is just one thing I must be sure of," he said. "Captain Andrews told me he was sending me—not a boy—but a real man! Are you a real man?"

Peter again thought of his father and what he had told him. "Very soon you must be ALL man, and show everyone what a fine man you can be." Peter squared his slim shoulders and announced in a firm, clear voice, "I AM THAT MAN!"

"He certainly will be!" added his mother. All three laughed with pleasure, even though Peter had to turn away quickly so no one could see his eyes. Men did not cry—children did—and he was no longer a child.

Peter, the boy in this story, was John Peter Zenger. He came to America in 1710 when New York was one of 12 British colonies.

Peter grew up to become a printer, and publisher and editor of his own newspaper, the *New York Weekly Journal*.

At that time, a law made it illegal for anyone to criticize the government. But Zenger believed that every citizen had the right to read the truth about bad government. So he began to print true stories about the dishonesty of the New York government.

Angry government members accused Zenger of printing lies. They had him arrested and jailed.

At Zenger's trial, Andrew Hamilton, his lawyer, argued that no one could be sent to prison for printing the truth about the government. The jury agreed, and freed Zenger, who became famous as a defender of freedom of the press.

An early American printing press

More To Read

Peter Zenger, Fighter for Freedom by Tom Galt. Published by Thomas Y. Crowell Company, New York, 1951.

Seven Famous Trials in History by Robin McKown. Published by Vanguard Press, New York, 1963.

Biographical Table

This table is an alphabetical listing
of famous people in this volume.
It tells when the people lived,
where they were born, and why they are famous.

Name	Born-Died	Birthplace	Why Famous	Page
René Laënnec	1781-1826	Quimper, France	Invented the stethoscope	8
Marquis de Lafayette	1757-1834	Chavaniac, France	Military leader in American Revolutionary War and French Revolution	16
Harry Lauder	1870-1950	**Portobello, Scotland** (now part of Edinburgh)	Entertained audiences with character sketches and Scottish-dialect songs	22
Abraham Lincoln	1809-1865	Near present-day Hodgenville, Kentucky	The 16th President of the United States	28
Charles A. Lindbergh	1902-	**Detroit, Michigan**	Made first nonstop solo flight across Atlantic Ocean in 1927	34
Sir Thomas Lipton	1850-1931	Glasgow, Scotland	Yachtsman and businessman	40
Sir Joseph Lister	1827-1912	Upton, Essex, England	Founded antiseptic surgery	46
Joe Louis	1914-	Lexington, Alabama	Heavyweight boxing champion, 1937–1949	54
Connie Mack	1862-1956	East Brookfield, Massachusetts	Great manager in baseball history—helped organize the American League	60
Sir Alexander Mackenzie	*1764-1820	Island of Lewis, off coast of Scotland	Canadian trader and explorer who discovered Mackenzie River	68
Francis Marion	*1732-1795	Berkeley County, South Carolina	American general in Revolutionary War	76
Robert B. (Bob) Mathias	1930-	Tulare, California	Won the national and Olympic decathlons in 1948 and Olympic decathlon in 1952	84
Wolfgang Amadeus Mozart	1756-1791	Salzburg, Austria	Wrote musical masterpieces	100
James A. Naismith	1861-1939	Almonte, Ontario, Canada	Invented the game of basketball in 1891	108
Napoleon Bonaparte	1769-1821	Ajaccio, Corsica	Emperor of the French who created an empire that covered most of western and central Europe	116
Florence Nightingale	1820-1910	Florence, Italy	Founded the nursing profession	124
Annie Oakley	1860-1926	Patterson Township, Ohio	Expert shot—star in Buffalo Bill's Wild West Show	132
Louis Pasteur	1822-1895	Dôle, France	Scientist who made major contributions to chemistry, medicine, and industry	160
Robert Peary	1856-1920	Cresson, Pennsylvania	Discovered the North Pole	166

Name	Born-Died	Birthplace	Why Famous	Page
Pheidippides	*510-490 B.C.	Ancient Greece	Ran from Marathon to Athens, about 25 miles, to deliver a message that saved the city of Athens	174
Molly Pitcher	1754-1832	Near Trenton, New Jersey	Heroine of Revolutionary War	182
Pocahontas	*1595-1617	Near Jamestown, Virginia	Saved the life of Captain John Smith, the leader of the settlers in Jamestown, Virginia	190
Marco Polo	*1254-1324	Venice, Italy	His stories of his travels in central Asia and China gave Europe the first real information about the Orient	198
John Wesley Powell	1834-1902	Mount Morris, New York	Geologist who led the first expedition down the canyons of the Green and Colorado rivers in 1869	214
Pierre Radisson	*1636-1710	France	French explorer and fur trader in North America	222
Paul Revere	1735-1818	Boston, Massachusetts	American patriot who carried news to Lexington of the approach of British soldiers, April, 1775	230
Jackie Robinson	1919-	Cairo, Georgia	First Negro player in modern American major-league baseball	238
Will Rogers	1879-1935	Near Oologah, Indian Territory (now Oklahoma)	Stage and motion-picture star, and noted homespun philosopher	244
Babe Ruth	1895-1948	Baltimore, Maryland	Considered the greatest slugger in base-ball history	252
Sacagawea	*1787-1812	Idaho	Principal guide and interpreter for Lewis and Clark Expedition to Pacific Ocean, 1804—1805	260
Albert Schweitzer	1875-1965	Kaysersberg, Alsace	German physician, philosopher, musician, clergyman, missionary, and writer on theology	286
Robert Falcon Scott	1868-1912	Devonport, England	English explorer who reached the South Pole in 1912	292
Sequoyah	*1770-1843	Taskigi, Tennessee	Invented a system of writing for the Cherokee Indians	302
Robert Louis Stevenson	1850-1894	Edinburgh, Scotland	One of the world's most popular poets and writers—wrote *Treasure Island*	310
John Sutter	1803-1880	Baden, Switzerland	Founded New Helvetia, now Sacramento, California, in 1839	318
Booker T. Washington	1856-1915	Hales Ford, Virginia	Negro educational leader	342
Frank Lloyd Wright	1869-1959	Richland Center, Wisconsin	Noted American architect	348
John Peter Zenger	1697-1746	Germany	Fought for freedom of the press in early America	356

*Approximate dates

Illustration
Acknowledgments

The publishers of CHILDCRAFT gratefully acknowledge the courtesy of the following artists, photographers, publishers, agencies, and corporations for illustrations in this volume. Page numbers refer to two-page spreads. The words "(*left*)," "(*center*)," "(*top*)," "(*bottom*)," and "(*right*)," indicate position on the spread. All illustrations are the exclusive property of the publishers of CHILDCRAFT unless names are marked with an asterisk (°).

Index to Volume 13

Use this index to find the authors, the major characters, and the subjects of the stories in this volume. The authors' names are in italics. To find the title of a story, look at the Table of Contents in the front of the book.

A general index to CHILDCRAFT appears in Volume 15.